GENERATIONS OF THE DEAD...

Michael Henry Brown

BROADWAY PLAY PUBLISHING INC
New York
www.broadwayplaypublishing.com
info@broadwayplaypublishing.com

GENERATIONS OF THE DEAD IN THE ABYSS OF CONEY ISLAND MADNESS
© Copyright 1993 Michael Henry Brown

All rights reserved. This work is fully protected under the copyright laws of the United States of America. No part of this publication may be photocopied, reproduced, stored in a retrieval system, or transmitted, in any form or by any means, electronic, mechanical, recording, or otherwise, without the prior permission of the publisher. Additional copies of this play are available from the publisher.

Written permission is required for live performance of any sort. This includes readings, cuttings, scenes, and excerpts. For amateur and stock performances, please contact Broadway Play Publishing Inc. For all other rights please contact the author's estate c/o B P P I.

Cover photo by T Charles Erickson
I S B N: 978-0-88145-105-4
First edition: May 1993
This edition: May 2017
Book design: Marie Donovan
Typeface: Palatino

ORIGINAL PRODUCTION

GENERATIONS OF THE DEAD IN THE ABYSS OF CONEY ISLAND MADNESS was first produced at the Hammerstein Center of Columbia University. It was subsequently optioned by Crossroads Theater in 1988, and workshopped in the Mark Taper Forum's TaperLab '88 and at the Ensemble Studio Theater.

The play premiered on 2 November 1990 at the Long Wharf Theater in New Haven, CT (Arvin Brown, Artistic Director, and M Edgar Rosenblum, Executive Director). The cast and creative contributors were as follows:

REED	Isiah Washington
LENA	Kimi 'Sung
LENORE	Lorey Hayes
JOB	William Jay Marshall
CODY	Jeff Caldwell Williams
THE BUTTERMAN	Jerome Preston Bates
MARLENE	Petie Trigg Seale
Director	L Kenneth Richardson
Set design	Donald Eastman
Costume design	Judy Dearing
Lighting design	Anne Militello
Sound design	Rob Gorton
Fight director	David Leong
Production stage manager	Ruth M Feldman

Subsequently, the play was produced at Penumbra Theater in St Paul, MN.

CHARACTERS

LENORE: A black woman of 34, who may look a few years older because of her previous street life. She is an attractive woman despite the hardness and is "stacked" as they say.

CODY COOPER: He is an intelligent, educated 20-year-old black. There is a bit of the snob about him. He is a student actor.

MARLENE COOPER: CODY's mother. She is 52. She is wheelchair-bound because of a recent stroke.

REED: CODY's friend. LENORE's son. LENA's twin brother. He is 18.

LENA: A younger, smaller version of her mother. She is CODY's girlfriend.

JOB: LENORE's second husband. Not the father of LENA and REED; the alleged father of at least one of LENORE's other children. He is 53.

BUTTERMAN: A hustler. Hustles anything and anyone. A ladies' man. Tall, handsome, and cryptic. Throughout the play he is never without dark shades. He is 35.

TIME: The present

PLACE: The Coney Island section of Brooklyn. Long Island.

ACT ONE
Prologue

(The main setting of the play is an apartment in the Poseidon housing projects in the Coney Island section of Brooklyn. A claustrophobic living room and dining area are visible. Upstage center is a row of windows that stretches from the dining room area to the living room area. Through the windows can be seen a sunless, moonless sky. The lighting simply differentiates day or night. Through the center window, in the distance, is the Wonder Wheel. It is a gigantic Ferris wheel that is lit day and night. At various times during the play, the Wonder Wheel can be seen turning clockwise and counterclockwise. Downstage, there is the most expensive piece in the room, a floor-model color TV. It should be state-of-the-art and chic—perhaps a Sony with stereo. It should stand out more than the furniture, which is bland-looking in color and form. [Note: No Jesus, Martin Luther King, Kennedy brothers, We Shall Overcome paraphernalia should be hanging on the walls!] The dinette area is represented by a simple table with four chairs. Scenes in Long Island and Coney Island Amusement Park will be played out in the downstage areas in front of the apartment.)

(As the Prologue begins, lights rise on the area that represents the She-Ape exhibit in the amusement park. REED is dressed in a wizard's hat, a robe with stars, and a Daffy Duck T-shirt. His head is down, but when Jimi Hendrix's "Voodoo Chile" begins to play he slowly brings his head up until he is staring into the audience. He smiles.)

(Lights up on LENA in a parochial school outfit, staring straight ahead. Lighting shows the shadow of cage bars across her body.)

REED: Ladieeees and gentlemen...Transformation! Before ya eyes...I tell ya no lies. Square business...this is the serious,

serious, shit....Word the fuck up! An Amazon Mandinka mommy caged up. Why? Because of the curse of generations long dead. Caught in the abyss that drives us all to madnesss.... *Like all of us....* Inside her is brutality...a brutality that manifests itself into a five-hundred-pound ape!

(LENA *begins to gyrate and dance.*)

REED: The one that we all carry...the one that is the true foundation of our living souls.... (*He looks around.*) Do you doubt me? (*Lights flash around* LENA.) If I'm lyin' I'm flyin'.... (*He is now in front of* LENA.) She was found on an island...a princess...now we bring her to Coney Island, cage her so she can't escape.... There is no escape so forget your hope.... Step right up and watch this confused child turn, turn before your stoned-out, bloodshot eyes.

(LENA *starts to go into convulsions.*)

REED: Yes, yes, my fellow zombies, Darwin was right. We have all transformed.... And now you get to watch the wonder and horror of our transformation.

(*"Voodoo Chile" rises.*)

(LENA *is humping and grinding the air in a hysterical frenzy. She drops to the floor, possessed, humping and grinding the floor to the rhythm of the music. She yells, then the growl of an* APE *is heard.*)

(*Blackout*)

(*Music is low. Lights rise.* REED *stands where he was. But where* LENA *was now stands an* APE. *The transformation is complete.*)

REED: You comin' this way? You comin' to see this life we play? Then get up off the hope, Money!

(REED *begins to back up in fear. The* APE *approaches him from behind.*)

REED: There is our soul...our heart....
What we all hide in the dark....
And in this place...within this space...
There is no peace...only the Beast!

ACT ONE

And the Beast is us....
WORD!

(The APE *grabs* REED *from behind and begins to crush him.* REED *struggles as the lights go down and the music is in a frenzy.)*

(Blackout)

Scene One

(Late June. Lights rise on the apartment area. There is a bottle of Dewar's scotch on the coffee table, along with several bottles of Miller beer. These same items are on the dinette table, which has a deck of cards as well. LENORE *and her daughter,* LENA, *are on the couch.* LENORE *is rolling a joint. She takes a long drag, holds it in, then passes it to her daughter.* LENORE *takes a sip of scotch, then exhales her smoke. She takes a pack of Kools from the table and lights one. Meanwhile,* LENA *has been taking short drags on the joint. She passes the joint back to her mother. The passing of the joint goes on throughout the scene.* LENA *is wearing shorts and a halter top. Both are bare-footed.)*

LENORE: Shit...so god-damned hot...

LENA: Yo, Moms, I hear that....

LENORE: So is this beer. Damned Puerto Ricans sell you hot beer in the summer, cold beer in the winter...and us, like the fools we are, just keep buying it. This is what I'm talkin' bout...niggers don't stick together. I bet those guineas in Sheepshead Bay will blow a motherfucker's store up if he don't have no cold beer. Those "meeda-meeda" motherfuckers give us hot beer and the niggers just lap it up.

*(*LENA *gets up and goes to the kitchen.)*

LENORE: Bring me another one while you're in there.

*(*LENA *is heard in the fridge. She speaks the next lines from the kitchen.)*

LENA: It just seems hot because it's hotter than fridge can get cold. *(Pause)* Anyway, when I'm hot like this...nothing cools me off....

(LENA returns from the kitchen with two beers. She hands one to her mother, then sits beside her.)

LENORE: Speakin' of hot...how'd you and Cody last night?

(Pause)

LENA: I really don't want to get into this, Moms.

LENORE: Why the hell not? Girl, we put a lot of planning into last night. I didn't lend you my hottest nightie to hear you cryin' about wantin' to get into it. *(Pause)* So how'd you do?

LENA: He thought you might walk in on us.

LENORE: Most men I know find that a turn-on. Ain't he got no freak in him?

LENA: Cody doesn't work that way.

LENORE: How does he work?

LENA: Under proper conditions.

LENORE: Proper conditions? What kind of nigger is he?

LENA: He respects you.

LENORE: This ain't gettin' it girl. Do you know what to do when you're alone with him? It was a simple plan: get him hot and let nature take its course. *(Pause. She looks at LENA. She then pops open her beer and takes a sip.)* Do I have to show you what to do? Do you want to get this boy or what?

LENA: Moms, I really don't know if this is the right thing to do.

LENORE: Right thing to do? Just the other night you was down with it.... Oh, I done peeped your car, this is about the Butterman, huh?

LENA: Just leave the Butterman out of this. I've got my own mind.

LENORE: Fuck me to tears. Looka here, you can always have a Butterman. Hell, every other woman in Coney Island has.

ACT ONE

LENA: You don't gotta run down the history of the Butterman, I know the deal. I've got my own feelings about this.

LENORE: You know the deal, huh? Let me remind you that a man like the Butterman is in this world for two things: hustlin' and fuckin'.

LENA: See, Moms, you don't know nothing about the Butterman. You only see the money, the clothes, the flash...there's a lot more to him than that.

LENORE: I sure as hell ain't seen it, and I've known the Butterman ever since he was in his teens. Now you can screw the Butterman all you want, but wait till you get the deed to this lame Cody's ass.... Otherwise you're going to blow the real deal.

LENA: You don't understand, the Butterman makes me feel special.

LENORE: Is that what they call a good screw in Long Island?

LENA: I'm not talkin' about orgasms, Moms. I'm talking about feeling like you belong in this world. With the Butterman, I know who I am and where I belong. I just want to stay on the ground and hold on for dear life. When I'm with him I know I won't be floating away when I fall asleep. His arm is around my waist from the time I close my eyes until the time I open them again. Yeah, I don't float nowhere.

LENORE: Damn, he slingin' meat that heavy?

LENA: He's a heavy man.

LENORE: It's not like I don't understand the feeling of having a dude who can lay some pipe...but first you've got to get the ring through this boy's nose.

LENA: Sometimes I think I love Cody....

LENORE: Love ain't necessary to our plans.

(LENA *grabs a bag of reefer off the table and begins to roll a joint.*)

LENA: See, Cody, ever since I was a little girl, back in Long Island, he's made me float. When I was eight or nine, he used to make up stories just for me. Sometimes he would just tell me the story, but other times, it would be a real treat, he'd act out the whole story, and play every part. I loved it, Moms. It was better than TV. I was always the princess...and he would save me.

LENORE: Look, girl, you lost me. What the fuck are you talking about?

LENA: Cody has always made me float...and dream. I used to think that's the way it was supposed to be. But now, he scares me....

(LENA *passes the joint to her mother, who lights it and draws on it.* LENA *commences to roll another joint.*)

LENORE: No wonder he scares you...with this make-me-float make-me-dream bullshit! Man make you dream, you better be scared stupid. Cody's eyes remind me of your father's...Prince Charming sonofabitch...fairy-tale nigger, that's what he is. Now you're supposed to be pullin' him back to the ground with the rest of us. You don't let no man float you off to fairy tale land 'cause there ain't no such place.

(LENA *finishes rolling the second joint and lights it.*)

LENORE: I want you to appreciate the value of a lame like Cody.

LENA: I've got him on a leash.

LENORE: It don't sound like it to me. You just said the lame scares you. Now you're sayin' you got him on a leash, but it sounds to me like he could get a whiff of someone else. What's gonna stop him from doin' that, huh?

LENA: Me.

LENORE: Shit. I've sent my kids off to camp so you can get the deed to this boy's ass. You got that whole room to yourself and you can't suck him in? It ain't nothin' to gettin' pregnant....

LENA: I know that, Moms....

LENORE: The question is, are you going to get pregnant?

LENA: I'm trying to tell you, but you are not listening....

ACT ONE

LENORE: I'm listening, Sweetheart....

LENA: I don't know if getting pregnant is something I want to do.

LENORE: I can understand that.

LENA: You can?

(LENORE *pours a shot of the scotch for* LENA *too.*)

LENORE: *(Handing drink to* LENA*)* Of course I do. *(She takes her drink and throws it back in one gulp.)* But you have to understand that a lame like Cody will give you anything you want.

LENA: The Butterman gives me anything I want.

LENORE: I know he does, Baby....

LENA: Shoot, he's got sixty grand in his pocket right now.

LENORE: I hear that.... But how much will he have tomorrow?

(Pause)

LENA: That's the life he leads.

LENORE: So, see, you understand that.... And what I'm talking 'bout here is the future, Baby.... You hook up Cody, and you'll get over like a fat rat.

LENA: Cody doesn't have a thing.

LENORE: But that crippled-bitch mother of his has a big house, money, cars....

LENA: None of it belongs to Cody.

LENORE: Look, the bitch gotta die sometime, right? She ain't got nobody but Cody.

LENA: She's not going anywhere anytime soon.

LENORE: What makes you so sure? She rolls around in that wheelchair all day long. She could accidently...wheel herself down a flight of stairs or somethin'....

LENA: Last time I was over there, she told me that if I tried to marry Cody, she'd disown him.

LENORE: I'm a mother. I know about motherhood. *(Slight pause)* The bitch is full of shit. She's gonna leave every dime to him. Look at the deal, Girl, you get knocked up and you have Marlene's first and only grandchild by her first and only son. It's a slick move.

LENA: I'm the one gettin' pregnant, Moms, I've got to think about this.

LENORE: Ain't nothin' to think about...

(JOB *enters the apartment with beer in hand.*)

JOB: Hell is hot tonight.

(He looks at the two women on the couch. They ignore him.)

LENORE: What the fuck are you lookin' at?

JOB: Yo Babes, you tell me?...'Cause I'll be damned if I know.

LENORE: Death.

JOB: I always knew death was an ugly bitch.

LENORE: I tell you one thing, Job...you damn-sight better be scared of this bitch.

JOB: I ain't afraid of your death.

(JOB *goes into his pocket and pulls out a wad of bills. He tosses it to* LENORE. *She begins to count the money.*)

LENORE: You comin' in here with your shit? I don't care how many drinks you had, you can't kick no ass in here.

JOB: I didn't come in here for no trouble, Babes, I just want somethin' to eat.

LENORE: You forget where the kitchen is?

(JOB *looks at them for a second, then goes to the kitchen.*)

LENORE: It's too hot for his bullshit tonight. *(She finishes counting the money.)* Damn, Job, next time you bring your check home first, then I'll give you money to go drinkin'.

LENA: He spent a lot, Moms?

LENORE: Nah, I'm just keepin' him in check. Gotta pay the rent and some other things...

ACT ONE 9

LENA: I hear that.

LENORE: Do you really?

LENA: Yeah, Moms.

LENORE: Then why ain't y'all givin' me some money from this She-Ape job? It's time for y'all to bring some food in here.

LENA: The She-Ape is a dead job. I'm glad I'm not on tonight. They're using that white girl. The customers don't believe I turn into an ape.

LENORE: Suckers always want to believe.

LENA: But Cody is such a terribly unconvincing ape.

LENORE: Is he all that bad? All he's got to do is wear the monkey suit.

LENA: Yeah, well, Cody be a trip. He's so determined to play the ape with class and dignity...a "positive and uplifting performance" as he puts it. After the transformation, when he jumps into the audience, the customers don't run...they laugh.

LENORE: And he's going to acting school how long?... Can't fuck...can't act...what can he do?

(They laugh. Noise is heard coming from the kitchen. JOB comes out to the dining area and places a plate of chicken and cabbage on the table. He goes into the kitchen.)

LENORE: I'm serious, that boy sounds as helpless as a child. That's why I know you can hook him up before he knows what happened.

LENA: But what if his mother does disown him? Then where does that leave us?

LENORE: What's the worst that could happen? You just do what that girl on the eighth floor did: Just go the welfare and tell them you're pregnant...tell 'em you have no idea who the daddy is....

LENA: I'll look like a slut....

LENORE: Hell, they'll probably set you up in one of those duplexes on Neptune Avenue.... Then you make the fool quit college and this actin' shit....

LENA: But acting and school, those are Cody's loves...and what I love about him.

LENORE: See, now I got caught in that trick-baby with your father. Don't you let him do you like your father did me. He had two loves too, his saxophone and his dope.

(Frantic shutting of cabinet drawers and doors is heard coming from the kitchen.)

LENORE: Now Job, see, he works. Job don't want nothin' but a job and a place to lay his head, and....

JOB: *(From the kitchen)* Hot sauce!

(Pause)

LENORE: A man that don't want much is more inclined to dote on a woman.... Word! His only ambition is you.

(A loud crash is heard from the kitchen.)

JOB: God damn it! *(He comes out into the dining area.)* What I tell you? How many times do I have to tell you?... You're stupid—stupid! I can't live in a house like this....

LENORE: What the hell is wrong with you?

JOB: Lenore, did you go shopping or what?

LENORE: Yesterday... You know that.

JOB: No hot sauce...no mayonnaise...

LENORE: Praise the Lord you got food.

JOB: What the hell good is food without hot sauce...without mayonnaise? *(Pause)* Dumb bitch.

LENORE: All right, Job.

(LENORE looks at LENA, then rises from the couch and goes past JOB, and into the kitchen. JOB sits to eat. LENA begins rolling another joint.)

JOB: Your mother is a dummy, Lena. She ain't got sense God gave a goat. I don't ask for much, but I refuse to eat in

ACT ONE

a house without hot sauce or mayonnaise. All these years, all these god-damned years!

(LENORE *comes out of the kitchen with a large jar of mayonnaise and a meat cleaver. She stands behind the sitting* JOB.)

JOB: She goes shopping and forgets the specialty of the man of the house. When I was in the Navy, they called that mutiny! The dumb bitch!

(LENORE *places the meat cleaver under* JOB's *chin. She slams the mayonnaise down on the table.*)

LENORE: You got problem?

JOB: Hey, Babes...I...I...just wanted a little mayonnaise...you know me.

(LENORE *puts her hand in the mayonnaise jar and scoops out a portion. She holds it in front of* JOB's *face. He is motionless.*)

LENORE: Is this enough?

JOB: Plenty, Babes.

(*With the meat cleaver still at his throat,* LENORE *spreads the mayonnaise all over his face.* JOB *is motionless.*)

LENORE: Now, I really did forget the hot sauce, but I'm sure I can come up with something hot and...red.

(*She kisses the top of his head, then buries the cleaver into the table.* JOB *reacts to the impact.*)

LENORE: Enjoy your meal.

(*Without wiping the mayonnaise from his face,* JOB *begins eating.* LENORE *goes back to the living room and sits with* LENA, *who passes her the joint.* LENORE *holds out her hand, and* LENA *slaps her "five".*)

LENA: You know how to deal, Moms.

LENORE: You think so?

LENA: You know it.

LENORE: Then why don't you listen to me?

LENA: I listen to you, Moms.

LENORE: No you don't. Otherwise you'd see where I was comin' from with this Cody thing.

LENA: I told you, Moms. I've got to think about it.

LENA: I don't think there's much to think about.

(LENA *picks up her shot of scotch and goes to the window and looks out.*)

LENORE: Oh, it's like that, is it?

LENA: It ain't like nothing, Moms. I just need to think things out.

(LENA *takes a sip of her drink.*)

LENORE: Yeah, you do that, but I want you to understand where I'm coming from...I'm your mother. Okay, I didn't raise you...but it's my obligation to make sure you step into life on the good foot. This is life.

(LENORE *takes a drag on the joint.* LENA *downs her drink. Lights fade on the two women as* JOB *continues to eat, then black as the Wonder Wheel spins.*)

Scene Two

(*Lights up on the Coney Island She-Ape area.* REED *stands mesmerized by his own humming of Billie Holiday's "God Bless the Child". He is deeply into this—it is as if his humming is part of an instrument in a band. He finishes and smiles.* CODY *enters in his ape suit. He has his mask in hand.*)

CODY: You ready to blow this joint?

REED: I'm blown.

CODY: Oh, man, come on... (*Pause*) Is there a day that goes by when you're not like this?

(REED *jerks and twitches.*)

CODY: This is fucked up, Man, this is really fucked up.

REED: Wow!... Colors...you should see 'em Cody.... This is going to be a nice trip.

ACT ONE

CODY: Yeah, well, I've seen all the colors....

REED: Not like these...

CODY: ...and they're horrible illusions. I don't know how you do it every day.

REED: If you could see, Cody, if you could only see.

CODY: See? Yeah, that shit had me seeing fucking tigers.

REED: *(Laughs)* It was a black and orange Corvette.

CODY: Looked like a fucking tiger to me. That shit had me hugging walls.

(REED *continues to laugh.*)

CODY: It wasn't funny, Reed.

REED: I had to peel you off the wall.

CODY: It's not funny, I thought I was going to die.

REED: You should try it again...once you get the hang of it, it's like a dream you control...a fairy-tale nightmare.

CODY: I once read about these guys on acid who went on the grass to look at the sun...to stare at the fucking sun.... And they did, Reed. They looked at the sun until it burned their eye sockets out....

REED: Would you put a freeze on that shit?

CODY: One day you may decide to have a child...what are you going to say to your wife when she gives birth to a twelve-pound baby eyeball?

REED: Man, man, you're really fucking with my head.

CODY: Yeah, well, that's just the way I felt when you gave me some of that blotter. I felt like everybody was fucking with my head.

REED: It's not my fault you couldn't handle it. It's not like somebody forced it on you. See, you can't deal with anything or anybody that makes you dig yourself. That's why you have this contempt for the Butterman.

CODY: I have contempt for Butterman because he's scum.

REED: Man, why you gotta dis' the Butterman like that?

CODY: Because of what he represents. Don't you understand? Butterman kills people. It's people like him that make the Coney Islands. Can't you see that?

REED: Who's Butterman killing?

CODY: For starters, he's killing this guy I grew up with. A guy just like me. A guy who should know better than to fall for his street philosophy bullshit.

REED: Yo, man Cody, would you cool the fuck out? You're doin' a job on my head.... Snatched me out of this caravan on the way to Timbuktu with Africans, Arabs, Asians.... *(He goes off into a daze.)*

CODY: Would you come back to reality?

REED: Now, check this out. We've been closed for an hour and a half, it's ninety-five degrees, and you're standing there in that monkey suit...and you're asking me to come back to reality?

CODY: Look, I want to ask you something.

REED: Yeah, what?

CODY: Are you going to come with me when I get Lena out of C.I.?

REED: What makes you think I want to go anywhere with you? What makes you think Lena wants to go anywhere with you?

CODY: Would you just answer my question?

REED: I ain't never goin' back to my aunt's...the way she dogged us for wantin' to know who our moms was and shit....

CODY: You don't have to. I was thinkin' of someplace different for the three of us.

REED: Oz, Cody...I've always wanted to groove on Oz.

CODY: No, no, California... Just imagine the three of us setting up house near a beach. Reed, you can have your own room, all to yourself, nobody bugging you.... You can cool out and go to the beach....

ACT ONE   15

REED: I live in Coney Island...I can go to the beach every day.

CODY: I'm talking the Pacific Ocean. A real ocean. Listen, Reed, we'll get you a sax...you've always wanted to learn sax. Well, you can play all day and night.... You can go to the beach and blow while the ocean is your rhythm section. And Lena can go to college, and we'll come home in the evening and we'll go for long drives down the coast...the three of us.... We'll go down to Mexico.... We'll have a life that is so removed from this shit.... See, we need a place where we can grow.... My acting teacher thinks I'm ready for movies and stuff...he's thinking the city, but I say why not L.A.? Movies and stuff....

REED: We're off to see the Wizard....

CODY: Do you understand what I'm saying? It's time I left home.... I can understand why you don't want to go back to your aunt...but this isn't you...it isn't Lena.... No disrespect to your mother, but, Reed, this is Niggersville....

REED: Lions and tigers and niggers...oh, my...

CODY: We were brought up special.... We can have anything we want.... We were taught that...and it's the fucking truth....You've been out here a year...and you've picked up the ways...but this isn't you.... It isn't Lena.... So let's get out of here before it's too late....

REED: Yo, Cody, that's deep....

CODY: You like that idea?

REED: Yeah, you, me, and Lena...in Oz... Get to wear ruby slippers and shit...drop houses on bitches...get blown away in poppy fields, fly with some monkey... Whoa! The colors... MGM Techno-blotter-color!!

CODY: Here I am telling you my plans for us...but it's the Butterman again...that shit he feeds you to take and sell.... I'm telling you a dream for us that we can make a reality... and you're off somewhere...out of your fucking head. I could kill the Butterman.... I'm going to get you out of here, even if I have to kill him.

REED: You gonna kill the Butterman? Yo, straight up, I tell you this in all sincerity and clarity, you get in the way of the Butterman and he'll cut you every which way but loose. Check it, word up, don't cross him.

CODY: So much respect for a low-life dealer.

REED: He's the king of Coney Island.

CODY: I could do what the Butterman does with my eyes closed. If he's the King of Coney Island then I'm the God of Brooklyn.

REED: You hustle? I can't imagine you scramblin'. Now your pops...there was a man....

CODY: Shut the fuck up about my father...

REED: I'm only saying....

CODY: You don't know anything about it. People like the Butterman and some of these sleaze bags...they are shit.... Never even think that my father was anything like this. You knew him better than that, Reed, he loved you, he'd come out of his grave and haunt you....

REED: Right, I don't know shit. I'm just trying to give you a warning about the Butterman. I don't know who the fuck you think you are to judge him. He doesn't judge you. The man actually digs you.

CODY: What the fuck does he like me for?

REED: Maybe he thinks you're his long-lost son.

(REED *laughs.* CODY *does not.*)

REED: He's always asking about you.

CODY: And do you know why he asks about me?... Because he knows, that I know, that he ain't shit. The first time I saw him, I said to myself, "Cody, there goes a real-life, genuine motherfucker!"

(REED *begins to laugh. The* BUTTERMAN *enters, dressed in a designer silk suit, and wearing dark shades that he never takes off during the course of the play.* REED, *in his acid-inspired laughing fit, does not notice him. In the background, the Miles Davis*

ACT ONE 17

version of "'Round Midnight" is heard. BUTTERMAN *and* CODY *exchange steely glares.)*

BUTTERMAN: Why do I get the feeling there's some kind of shit lingering in the air?

CODY: Did you change your Pamper today?

BUTTERMAN: Boy, you just don't know. I like you...you should remember that.

CODY: What the fuck does that mean?

(BUTTERMAN *smiles at* CODY. *He walks over to* REED, *who has finally stopped laughing. Exhausted,* REED *has his head in his hands.)*

BUTTERMAN: You cool?...You all right, Partner?

(REED *suddenly pops up like a jack-in-the-box.)*

REED: Got a hold of my feet, my legs, my hands, my heart, my soul...I'm dead....

BUTTERMAN: Now you're talkin' like Reed.

REED: He's in here somewhere.

(BUTTERMAN *opens his briefcase and pulls out a large paper bag.)*

CODY: Not today, Butterman.

BUTTERMAN: Say what?

CODY: Reed's saying no today.

BUTTERMAN: Oh, you one of them just-say-no motherfuckers.

CODY: Just close up your bag... Reed is through....

BUTTERMAN: What's he yip-yappin' about, Reed?

REED: Follow the yellow brick road...

CODY: Why don't you just leave him alone...can't you see that shit's eating his brain out?

BUTTERMAN: He's just diggin' himself, Homeboy.

CODY: Let's get one thing straight, I am not your homeboy.

BUTTERMAN: You know what? You're absolutely right, but you may be the next lame-ass sucker I kill.

(Pause)

REED: So what we got?

BUTTERMAN: Upstroke, downstroke, a crack of dawn's early light in the pit of darkness...and, a little bit of that heaven you're on now.

REED: Yo, yo... *(He laughs.)* I've been trippin' out on death, and I realized...realized...realized....

BUTTERMAN: Let me dig it, Cool...

REED: ...death is all around us.

BUTTERMAN: That's why we get along, Reed, our heads are in the same place.... I was trippin' just the other night with uhh...uhh.... *(Pause. He looks at* CODY, *then laughs.)* Ain't that somethin'? I forgot who she was.... But I started diggin' the past. I'm talkin' 'bout before I was born.... Now this chick, that I can't remember, she was sittin' on top of me just workin' away...screamin'...and where do you think my head is at? In the past. When I was split in two. Joy juice in my pops...and egg in my moms. It was the serious.... Don't you ever wish you could go back into the past, like before you were born?

CODY: Yeah, Butterman, I wish I could go back before any of us were conceived.

BUTTERMAN: Now, that's a trip. What would you do, Youngblood?

CODY: I'd give your father a box of scumbags.

(Silence. The BUTTERMAN *smiles.* REED *begins to laugh. The* BUTTERMAN *laughs with him. The* BUTTERMAN *pulls out his switchblade.)*

(Pause)

REED: Ig' him for me...okay?

BUTTERMAN: I'm supposed to ignore a mouth full of disrespect from some bourgeoise nigger-child from Long-fucking-Island?

CODY: You mean the big, bad, Butterman can't take me without a knife?

ACT ONE 19

BUTTERMAN: Who do you think you're fuckin' with? I want to brand you, Bitch, so you'll remember me for the rest of your life...every time you look in the mirror....

REED: C'mon, Butterman, cool out!... What would Malcolm say?

BUTTERMAN: Reed, I dig you like a little brother, but you try and run some psych shit on me and I just may cut your throat.

REED: I ain't runnin' no game.... But isn't this what he was talkin' against?... Brothers killin' brothers?... I've read the books and listened to the records at your crib. You taught me.

(BUTTERMAN *draws closer to* CODY.)

BUTTERMAN: That ain't got jack-shit to do with this.

REED: You've said it yourself...that Cody's got a future.... Now you're gonna cut him because he slung a few words?

(Pause. BUTTERMAN *puts the blade away. He then gets in* CODY's *face.* CODY *nervously stands his ground.*)

BUTTERMAN: There was this time when John Coltrane....

CODY: Who?...

BUTTERMAN: John Coltrane... You a college boy...an artist...you know who the fuck he is....

CODY: Of course...

BUTTERMAN: John Coltrane was playin' for Miles, and if you say "Miles who?" we gonna rumble.... Anyway, this was in the fifties, before 'Trane made it really big...and they're playin' at this club...and they're groovin' on this number, everybody is takin' their solo...and then it's 'Trane's turn...'Trane goes for it...he tears the joint up...got the whole joint mesmerized.... Then the band finishes the song...everybody is applauding...and they get ready to get off the stage for the break, when Miles walks straight up to 'Trane and pops him right in the gut.... Out of nowhere. 'Trane just keels over, and Miles walks off. Now I think it was Thelonious Monk, who had been in the audience, who told 'Trane to come play for him. That he didn't have to take that kind of shit off nobody, not even Miles. 'Trane left Miles...and Miles didn't like this...in fact it hurt him, because he loved 'Trane...even though he hurt him, he loved him. And 'Trane knew it...'cause he eventually came back to play with Miles...but by then he was too big...even for Miles.... See, 'Trane had always been bigger than Miles spiritually, that's why he didn't respond to the punch in the stomach.... When he came back to the band he was bigger musically.... So you can say an ass kickin' made 'Trane bigger and better than Miles.... 'Trane took it, the punch in the gut, and made it into something that he kept in his art.... I dig Miles...but he's an angry man.... Hey, I can dig it, know what I mean?... But if he'd put that anger into his horn...see, the pain is there...but I don't get the anger... and I think that's because he's taken it out on loved ones. But with 'Trane, it's all there.... Just listen to "Alabama"... Whew! Miles could never do some shit like that because he can't trap his anger in his horn and mix it up with all those other feelings.... *(Pause)* I like what you're doin', boy. School, actin'...positive shit... But unfocused emotions can kill you....

CODY: You think I'm worried about you killing me?

BUTTERMAN: Reed, this Motherfucker hasn't heard a word I said. Dude, I ain't got to kill you. Keep hangin' 'round here and you're gonna get devoured. That is if some broad don't get your balls first. *(Pause)* You don't belong. *(Pause)* Consider yourself lucky.

(BUTTERMAN *gives* REED *the bag of drugs.* REED *pulls out a wad of bills and gives them to* BUTTERMAN.)

BUTTERMAN: Catch you on the rebound, Reed.

("'Round Midnight" rises slowly. BUTTERMAN *takes one more look at* CODY *and laughs. Then he leaves.)*

REED: The man is a walking case of dynamite and you want to light his fuse?

CODY: He's nothing but a coked-out bluff.

REED: Who would kill your ass in a fly's heartbeat.... You're the educated one. You heard the brother speak. Can't you understand where he's comin' from....

ACT ONE 21

CODY: Cokehead city.

REED: Man, listen to what he's sayin'.... He's got an ace up his sleeve but it won't come out.... It's gonna take somethin' big for it to come out again...but he's got to beard it with the illusion.... But one day he's gonna get up off it...he's gonna step off...and then you're gonna see the real deal, Cody.... The spirit that was held within...the great booga mooga.... Then you'll know...then you'll know....

CODY: Know what?

REED: That it was an illusion...a front...until he could get it together and rise again.... Word!

CODY: Oh, now I see what you do...you get tripped out, go to his house, listen to Coltrane records, and look at his Malcolm posters...and then you're convinced he's deep. A second-rate hustler...

REED: I remember your pops....

CODY: What about my father?...

REED: He used to play Coltrane, Miles, Monk, when we was little.... Used to dig him in his den...with his scotch, kicked back in his easychair, in his smoking jacket... wearing his favorite shades. *(Slight pause)* Do you think, if we'd of asked him, he'd broke down jazz to us the way the Butterman has to me?

CODY: Look, man, I don't want to hear any of this nonsense.

REED: I'm just tryin' to make a point about your....

CODY: There is no point to make. Just do me a favor, don't bring up my father in the context of this bullshit.

REED: I'm diggin' myself all the time. P. What about you? I've got a little acid here that will let you dig yourself all the way live...if you can stand it...which we both know you can't....

CODY: You're just losin' yourself, Man.... Why don't you think about California.... I can make it happen.... You'll be out of the shit. Don't you want to be out of the shit?

REED: Don't you?

CODY: One day it's going to be so clear. We're going to be in the sun. This is going to be the distant past. You, me, and Lena.

REED: And what about the baby?

CODY: Of course.

REED: Now I know you dippin' in the acid.... See, you only see what you want to see.... Nobody else's dreams are valid....

CODY: My dreams can become reality because they're not drug induced.... Yours could come true too...if you'd get off that stuff. You're turning into a fucking....

REED: Fuck you!

CODY: I'll talk to you when you come down off the space shuttle.

REED: I'm all for that. You comin' up to the crib?

CODY: I've got to drive out to see my mother. I haven't checked on her in a week. If I'm not back tonight, I'll see you in the morning.

REED: Oh, this is a cash run.

(CODY *smiles.* REED *reaches into his pocket and pulls out keys that belong to* CODY.)

REED: Can't fly that Mazda without those.... Me...me...myself...and I, I, I...gonna check out....

CODY: Reed, think about what I said...my plan...we can do it...the three of us could be happy.... *(He looks at the unsteady* REED.*)* You okay?

REED: No. *(Pause)* I need to drop another tab...then maybe I'll get some peace tonight. That's all I really want.

(They give each other a "high five", then CODY *leaves.* REED *reaches into the bag that* BUTTERMAN *gave him and takes out a tab of acid. He is about to place it on his tongue as the lights go down.)*

ACT ONE   23

Scene Three

(Midnight. JOB, LENA, LENORE, and the BUTTERMAN are at the dinette table playing cards. REED is sitting on the floor watching TV. The light from the set is reflecting on him, but there is no sound. The Wonder Wheel is lit up against the night sky. JOB rises out of his seat with a playing card in his hand. He raises it over his head and slams it down on the table, hard.)

JOB: Your asses are dead now. Run it!

(JOB collects the cards. They toss more cards from their hands on the table. JOB slams another card down on the table, hard.)

JOB: *(To* LENA*)* We got 'em, Partner. We're running a Boston on 'em.

LENA: It sure looks that way.

(LENORE throws the rest of her hand in.)

JOB: Pick that hand up and play it, Woman.

LENORE: You won, what the hell else do you want?

JOB: I want the pleasure of seeing this hand played all the way through.

BUTTERMAN: C'mon, Lenore, pick up your hand and play it through.

LENORE: You mind your fucking business or get the fuck out of my house.

LENA: C'mon, Moms...

LENORE: You mess with me and I'll send your ass straight to bed.

LENA: It's a little late for you to start raising me.

LENORE: Shut the fuck up!

(Pause)

BUTTERMAN: We're just sayin'....

LENORE: Hey, he won.

JOB: But playin' out a Boston is the climax, Babes.

(LENORE *walks away from the table.*)

LENORE: Yeah, well, you ain't gettin' your rocks off tonight.

(JOB *picks up the bottle of Dewar's from the table and pours himself a drink. He gulps it down and pours himself another.* BUTTERMAN *and* LENA *stare at each other.* LENORE *goes over to* REED.)

LENORE: Where's that boy at?

REED: I told you, Moms, he went to his mother's....

LENORE: You sure he didn't run off with that white girl y'all workin' with?

REED: Cindy? Why would you think that?

LENORE: Because he's just the type. Besides, your sister, the stupid bitch, is blowing it.

(BUTTERMAN *leans over the table to whisper something in* LENA's *ear.* LENORE *spots them.*)

LENORE: No whispering in my house god damn it.

BUTTERMAN: What?

LENORE: You're a guest in my house. House rules: No whispering...especially with my daughter.

BUTTERMAN: You sound ridiculous.

LENORE: You want ridiculous? What are you whispering about?

(*Pause*)

BUTTERMAN: I was just asking baby girl if she'd walk me to the store to get some more beer.

LENORE: It's midnight. They're closed.

JOB: No, Babes, there's that Spanish store on Mermaid...open twenty-four hours a day....

LENORE: How many times have I told you to stay out of people's business?

JOB: Look, Babes, I don't have to take this shit. I am the man of this house.

ACT ONE

(Pause. LENORE looks at him. He rises and goes to the bedroom area.)

BUTTERMAN: What's the harm in us going to the store?

LENORE: You know the rules of the house.

BUTTERMAN: Lenore, this is silly. Every time I want to walk out of the door with your daughter....

LENORE: You want her to walk with you to the store or what?

(BUTTERMAN pulls his briefcase from beneath the table and opens it.)

LENORE: How much?

BUTTERMAN: Sixty thousand.

LENORE: *(Whistles)* All yours?

BUTTERMAN: Who else's could it be? *(Pause)* The Butterman don't flunky for nobody.

LENORE: Big shit... Now the dope.

BUTTERMAN: I don't have any.

LENORE: Bullshit.

BUTTERMAN: All I have is my personal stash.

LENORE: Let's see it on the table.

(He takes out a vial of coke. He opens it and snorts a "one-on-one". LENA's eyes grow big. He starts to offer her some, but thinks better of it. He closes the vial, and places it on the table.)

LENORE: You get this back when you return with my daughter.

BUTTERMAN: *(Laughs)* You're crazy, Lenore. But that's why I like you.

LENORE: I'm crazy enough to know that you'd better have my daughter back here in fifteen minutes.

BUTTERMAN: We'll be right back. *(He goes over to REED.)* You mellow? *(REED just sits, staring at the TV)* Are you with us?

REED: I'm amongst the dead.

(BUTTERMAN *chuckles.*)

LENORE: Another thing, I don't want you giving my son any more of that shit.

BUTTERMAN: Nothin' to it...he's just diggin' himself.

LENORE: You think you're slick? Fuckin' with my son's head...fuckin' my daughter...just screwin' my twins...my first-born.

BUTTERMAN: Let's go, Baby girl... By the way, can I have some of my money back so I can buy some beer?

(LENORE *pulls a book of food stamps from her bosom. She hands them to* BUTTERMAN.)

BUTTERMAN: Food stamps! You tryin' to ruin my image?

LENORE: What are you talkin' about? It spend, don't it?... And while you're out there, get me a bag of smoke.

BUTTERMAN: Anything for the madame of the house.

BUTTERMAN: I ain't nobody's madame.... Look ahere, you fuck with me, and I'll burn your god-damned money.

(BUTTERMAN, LENA, *and* REED *laugh.*)

BUTTERMAN: Now that's some funny shit.

(BUTTERMAN *and* LENA *leave.* LENORE *takes a couple of snorts from the vial.*)

(*Pause*)

(*Then she takes some more. She puts the wad of money in her bosom, then thinks about it, and takes the money out. Looks around and goes into the kitchen.* REED *looks after her. He smiles. Then he stares at the screen. She returns, going directly over to* REED. *She looks at him watching TV.*)

LENORE: How the hell can you watch television without the sound?

REED: The wise man makes his own words.

LENORE: What do you get out of it?

REED: Peace.

(*Pause*)

ACT ONE 27

(LENORE *takes the remote and turns off the set.*)

REED: Yo, Moms, I was into it.

LENORE: Your sister and Butterman are goin' at it like bunnies.

(REED *covers his ears.*)

LENORE: Everybody in C.I. knows that.

(REED *shakes his head no.*)

LENORE: What are you? Blind?

REED: I wish I were.

LENORE: You're her twin, you speak to her.

REED: Not my function.

LENORE: This boy is going to come into some money one day...and every time he sees Lena his tongue laps up the ground she walks on.

REED: You can't run our lives.

LENORE: Never had the chance.

REED: I wonder whose fault is that?

(Pause)

LENORE: What? Like I had a choice or somethin'....

REED: Ain't that what life's about, Moms? Door number one or door number three? Sometime them choices is somethin' else, ain't they. We're talkin' about a real eenie, meenie, minee, moe type of decision.... I love the bastards.... I love them not.... I'll keep the bastards.... I'll keep them not....

LENORE: Reed, I'm the first to admit that I could have dealt with the whole situation a lot better....

REED: Gee, Moms...I wish I could say that is nice to know...but it's long too late for sacrifice.

LENORE: Sacrifice?... I was fifteen years old. What was I supposed to do?

REED: Chill.

LENORE: While your father ran around the country? What the fuck did I need him for? He wasn't there for me. So, I went out there and made my money. Nigger wasn't making shit. What did I need with a broke sax player? That's what I thought as I laid there in labor.... Laid there thinking it was all over...they hung that little bitch upside down, smacked her on the ass and shit, I'm relieved...ready for them to wheel me out...shit yeah! Then the doctor says, "Brace yourself, here comes another." Motherfucker you almost killed me. I was just a little thing. All by myself. Where the fuck was that dope-shootin', sax-playin' father of yours? I couldn't call my mother, God rest her soul, she had tried her best to stomp you and your sister out of me.... *(Silence)* Never saw you come out. Woke up and it was three days later. I had hemmorrhaged. Where the fuck was he? Blowin' that sax in a shootin' gallery in West Hell? See, a nigger can't be there when I need him, then I don't need the son of a bitch.

(REED *tries to turn the volume up on the TV.* LENORE *snatches the remote from him.*)

LENORE: I laid there thinkin' of how I almost died alone because I believed in some fairy tale-prince-charming-mother-goose-you-in-the-ass-bullshit!!! And I swore to myself I wouldn't be this fool again...not in this life.... So I was ripe when your father's mother and sister came to my hospital bed and said they'd take both of you.

REED: The faithful wait.

LENORE: The suckers wait.

REED: How would you know?

LENORE: What was I supposed to wait for?

REED: To nurse your babies...to hold them in your arms...to soothe their cryin'...to do the motherly thing...the motherly thing...to nurture...to take those first steps with them... to watch Dorothy and Toto with them for the first time... to hold them when the Wicked Witch looked too scary.... To hold their hands the first day of the rest of their lives... Something ordinary, Moms, something real.

LENORE: It don't get no more real than this.

ACT ONE

(REED *tries to turn on the TV;* LENORE *slaps his hand again.*)

REED: You almost killed me, Moms....

LENORE: What the fuck are you talkin' about?

REED: You almost killed me. I was just a little thing.... All by myself. Where the fuck were you, Moms?... I was all alone...in the dark.... Lena had left.... I couldn't call you, Moms.... 'Cause I didn't know what a mother was.... God rest your soul.... You did everything imaginable to kill us.... Lena was always stronger.... She fended for herself in the dark.... She was the first to get out.... I was trapped...the stench, Moms.... I could never breathe well in there...you made sure of that.... How did we survive all of those months?... The first time I got high...in you.... Why, Moms? Why? Lena was always stronger...from conception.... You really didn't want to kill her, did you? It was me, Moms. Wasn't it? Wasn't it me you were after? But your hatred made me strong...made me survive in your shit-filled womb.

LENORE: Boy, you better get up off this trippin' shit. You gonna trip out one day and never come-the-fuck-back. You can talk all of that okey-doke shit if you want.... But just you remember, you sprang from me, Bitch, so if I'm shit....

REED: I'm shit?

LENORE: You've got that right, Motherfucker! (*She goes to the kitchen table and picks up the vial of coke.*) You're right here in the shit with me...I'm your blood.

(REED *watches her as she goes to the window and looks out.*)

LENORE: Hot as a son of a bitch... All right now, they're takin' too long.... Butterman thinks he's gonna use my daughter as a fuck bunny? Right up under my nose? Well, I got something for his ass.... We got that lame Cody by the balls, and Butterman thinks I'm gonna let him fuck up my first-born's big chance.

(REED *turns up the TV volume.*)

LENORE: Reed, cut that shit down...I can hardly hear myself think.

(She turns back to looking out the window. REED *turns the volume up louder.* LENORE *turns back into the house.)*

LENORE: Did you hear what I said, you acid-brained Motherfucker?

(She goes back to looking out the window. Pause. He rises and goes to the window. He looks at her for a beat. Then he tries to push her out. She struggles her way out of the window. He now has his hands around her throat. After some tussling, she breaks free of him.)

LENORE: Motherfucker!

REED: Moms... Dear, sweet Moms. All these years that I dreamed of you, but never saw you.... Did you know that I used to search for you in the faces of other women?... But you were always here. *(He points to his heart.)* They'd tell me that when I was looking at Lena, I was looking at you.

(Pause)

(She takes a few steps back.)

REED: I'd pretend my pillow was your bosom, my blankets were your arms.... I never knew you, but I kept you alive. I believed in God then.... Now you stand there and call me a motherfucker? I'm the one who got screwed!!! *(Pause)* I kept you alive.... Look what you became.

(They stare at each other.)

(Lights fade on this tableau.)

Scene Four

(Lights rise on the bare stage down left. CODY *is in his ape suit. He is holding the mask.* MARLENE *is sitting in an electric wheelchair behind him.)*

MARLENE: I can't believe you, boy.... You've been living so uncivilized that....

CODY: I'm sorry, Ma....

MARLENE: Clean them...clean them right now...

ACT ONE

CODY: Okay, okay...

(CODY *wipes off the feet of his ape suit.*)

MARLENE: Tracking mud in my house...you know better than that.... You've just turned into a heathen. *(Thinking himself finished,* CODY *stands there.)* You're not finished, Boy. The floor.

(CODY *sighs and goes off.*)

MARLENE: You know how I feel about a clean house. When you were little you knew certain rooms were off limits to you...you knew not to go into the living room or the dining room....

(CODY *returns with a mop and begins mopping up his tracks.*)

MARLENE: ...and you always knew to clean your feet before stepping into this house. But now you come trampling in here like you're in a....

CODY: All right already. *(He goes with mop. Then returns quickly.)* So, how are you Ma?

MARLENE: How am I?... If you gave a good god damn, you'd be here.... But no, you'd rather be laying in a housing project with a bunch of no-account niggers.

CODY: You don't know them well enough to call them that.

MARLENE: I know the type very well.

CODY: Type? Type? What are you, Central Casting?

MARLENE: I'm not the only one that feels that way. Lena's aunt is the one that told me about them. She also thinks Lena's going to wind up breeding in those sardine cans.

CODY: Lena isn't anything like that, Ma. You know that.

MARLENE: Do I now?

CODY: Of course you do. How could you turn against her that way?

MARLENE: I don't think I've turned against her. She's the one who has changed.

CODY: She hasn't changed. Sure, she's going through changes, but she's still the little girl who used to help you in the garden when she was eight years old.

MARLENE: Honey, maybe you don't realize this, but people change, all the time. Sometimes...no matter what your upbringing, something happens so you find out who you are...and then you wallow in it.

CODY: Look, I'm the first to admit that Lena has let Coney Island influence her a bit...but it's temporary.... She never knew her mother, she's just trying to identify with her mother's world. That's all it is...

MARLENE: I'd like to believe that, but what I really think is that despite the years of separation, of never knowing a single breath or thought of her mother's, she's still a piece of the same meat.

CODY: Ma, if I didn't know you any better, I'd think maybe you were a snob.

MARLENE: A snob? You know where I came from...you know where your father came from.... We started at the bottom, like most of our folks do. Because I want to protect you I'm a snob? I know people like Lena's mother very well. I grew up with them.... Hell, I could have been one of them. But me, and your father, chose not to drown in the misery that surrounded us. We refused to sit and wait for death. I know people with three times the money that we have, and I wouldn't want you around them either. If I had one dollar in the bank, I would still be the person sitting in this wheelchair. Your father died an old man upstairs. You are all we had. Everything we built is yours. We bought this house...moved to this neighborhood, for you.... I've never told you that since you were small.... See, I've never told you this, but the doctors told me that I shouldn't have you. I had three miscarriages before you, and a baby girl who died at three weeks old. I had some physical problems, and the doctors told me I shouldn't ever try to get pregnant again. Your father was very sweet about it.... He told me it didn't matter, that he would love me, children or not.... But, see, I knew the importance of leaving a legacy to someone. What good would it be to have

ACT ONE

achieved so much and not leave it to someone, someone of your love, your body, to build on further? I was determined to have you...even if it threatened my very existence...and, also, I loved your father very much, he deserved to have someone carry his name. And so, we went to bed one night and we created you.... I thought of a boy all through it...a boy who could be anything he wanted to be if his mind was set on it. A boy who could use what we gave him as a modest foundation to a place we never imagined we could go. A snob? Fine then, I'm a snob. When it comes to you...protecting you...then I'm guilty as charged, damn it!

CODY: I'm not stupid, Ma. I understand all of that, but I love Lena. Is that so difficult to understand?

MARLENE: A piece of grief like Lena will give your children bad blood. You'll rue the day that you ever set eyes upon her.

CODY: I thought you loved Lena, Ma.... Three years ago, the two of you were in the garden getting your annual exhibit for your club. In the middle of designing the arrangements you had a stroke. Lena was there for you. She rode all the way to the hospital with you...held your hand.... She even nursed you when she wasn't in school. You know, deep down inside, what a good person she is....

MARLENE: I think that was somebody else. A very sweet child. The person you're talking about is just another ghetto strumpet.

CODY: Jesus, Ma.

MARLENE: Keep using the Lord's name in vain and hell will be your home for eternity.

CODY: You say god damn all the time.

MARLENE: I'm allowed, I'm a cripple. Her mother is a little street tramp. Don't you see? I don't want you anywhere near that world of whores and hustlers.

CODY: But Dad was a hustler.

MARLENE: Before you were born...

CODY: But, nevertheless, a hustler.

MARLENE: He didn't die in the streets...he didn't die a hustler, he got out before it got him. He died an old man right upstairs. He left that life just before you were born. We wanted to make sure you knew nothing of that world. Don't go romanticizing something you know nothing about. It wasn't a big thing. It just got us started. You don't know anything about that world so just forget about it. It was before your time....

CODY: I know that world.

MARLENE: You don't know anything about that world.

CODY: I know that world very well.

MARLENE: Why? Because you've spent a few weeks in Coney Island? You don't know anything about your father's world. It was before you were born.

CODY: I know his world. He took me to his world. It was our secret. *(Pause)* See, he never really quit hustling.

MARLENE: What are you talking about? He quit that world before you were born.... What are you trying to pull?

CODY: Sometimes we'd go driving...just driving around.... Sometimes we'd head toward Harlem.... I remember one occasion in particular.... We were cruising around and we stopped in front of this bar.... This woman comes out and sticks her head in his side of the car. Dad is real friendly to her, and they're laughing and joking. Then she reaches into her pocketbook and gives him several wads of cash. They laugh some more, and then she tries to kiss him, and he avoids it. She tries again, and he avoids again.... She looks at him for a moment and then she laughs at him. Dad was obviously stiff and uncomfortable from all of this. So she tells him, "Oh, you're acting uppity 'cause you've got your little bastard with you today." She walked away from the car and went into the bar. After a few seconds, Dad told me not to move, that he'd be right back. So Dad goes into the bar, and I just sit there.... After about five minutes the woman comes out of the bar, and toward the car. I notice that her nose is bleeding and her eye seems to be swelling. She comes over to my side of the car and leans over and

ACT ONE 35

says, "I'm sorry, Master Cooper, I didn't mean to call you a bastard, I didn't mean to disrespect you." Then she walks off. A few seconds later, Dad comes out of the bar. He tells me not to tell you where we were. Then he drives off as if nothing happened.... See, I know that world...far better than you think.

(Silence)

MARLENE: I think you're having some sort of fantasy. My goodness, I should have flushed you down the toilet. God is going to get you for this. You are the stupidest child God ever pumped breath into....

CODY: I'm just trying to make a point here, Ma....

MARLENE: My son was probably switched with you at birth. I bet he's a priest by now. He's at one with God.

CODY: God? Let me tell you something about your God. Your heaven. One day we won't exist. Forget about heaven...you're going to rot in the ground...and in a thousand years they'll plant a garden where you once had a grave...and maybe, just maybe your essence will have enriched the soil...and the richness of your essence will grow a big fat tomato...and some child will eat that tomato...and they will grow too. That's heaven, Ma...the only chance we've got at it...and you won't even be aware.

MARLENE: I don't believe you are saying this.... All of this because of this girl....

CODY: I'm going to be with Lena, Ma. It's as simple as that.

MARLENE: So, I guess that's final....

CODY: I am not going to let go of Lena.... She hasn't changed, she's just going through some changes...if you truly love someone you stand by them.

MARLENE: So I guess that means you're not going to be an actor.

CODY: Not to be an actor? What do you mean?

MARLENE: You're dedicating yourself to Lena. You're not going to have time for acting.

CODY: No. What are you talking about? To be on stage, Ma...you know how I feel. To create a whole other person for weeks...and then to get to be that person.... And then another show...another person... To be on the stage and to fool people into believing you're someone else.... When I'm up there I feel as if I'm actually in that world. That I'm somewhere else and someone else.... My acting teacher thinks I can go very far.... He thinks I've got the juice to go to Hollywood right now.

MARLENE: How are you going to Hollywood or anywhere else with Lena around your neck?

CODY: She'll be there to support me. She understands what I need. What I want.

MARLENE: Do you understand what she needs? What she wants?

CODY: Of course I do.

MARLENE: I think you're somewhere else. You're not here with the rest of us. You don't see things for what they are, but for what you want them to be.

CODY: I can make them what I want them to be.

MARLENE: Not in this world you can't. Or is it you can't admit to yourself what you really know...that this girl is no good.... Are you just fighting the facts? Fighting the facts doesn't mean you're going to change a thing.... Why don't you just stay here...relax, go to acting class, drive around... see other girls.... Just try it for a month... No contact with that girl...that world.... You can just float along...get yourself together.... I'll make your favorite dishes every day. You can forget about her for a short time, can't you? And we'll look at old movies like when you were small.... Come on, Cody, we can have some fun. I promise you, if Lena comes to that door I'll say you went away on a long trip.... Then you can watch her reaction...and then you'll know if this is for real at all.... How about it. If you want to know if this thing is for real you'll give it some time...and a test.... How about it, Cody?...Cody?...

(CODY *just stands there in silence, then puts on the mask and roars at her.*)

Scene Five

(Lights rise on the apartment. Baseball bat in hand, LENORE *is pacing.* LENA *is trying to calm her down.* BUTTERMAN *and* JOB *are at the dinette table.)*

LENA: Calm down, Moms.

LENORE: I'll calm that little son of a bitch up side his head.

LENA: It was the acid.

LENORE: Bullshit. That little bastard tried to kill me on the day he was born. He hated me from the womb.... You want him alive? Don't let him back in this house tonight. If you do, the little sucker will wake up dead.

JOB: Okay, Babes, just put the bat away.

(She lets LENA *take the bat away.)*

JOB: What did you do to that boy?

LENORE: I breathed, that's all the fuck I did.

JOB: Couldn't you have just kept your big mouth shut?

(Pause)

LENORE: Let me tell you something, the next time I hear you tell somebody to shut up in my house, I know an old bastard who is going to get his nuts cut off.

JOB: Look, Babes, I was only....

LENORE: Get out of this house.

JOB: Listen, Lenore, I pay the rent here....

LENORE: I bet you don't sleep your ass in here tonight...not alive.

JOB: I'm not leaving.

LENORE: Then get ready to rumble you jive-ass son of a bitch.

LENA: Go on, Job.

JOB: Where am I supposed to go this time of night?

LENA: Just take a long walk on the beach.... It's hot. Some of the breeze from the beach will cool you off.

JOB: You're wrong, Lenore...and you know it. We were just having a good time...like it used to be.... We used to sit all night and play cards, just you and me. And we'd have so much fun..... We'd pop popcorn...roast marshmallows.... The night used to seem like it went so quickly...before we knew it the sun was coming up...and we'd rush out to the beach and catch it rising.... It's like it never happened...like it was some movie I was watchin'.... Now the nights are long...they seem like they never end.... It's been better than this. You know that...and that's why you know you're wrong.

LENORE: I'm gonna put heat on your ass if you don't get out of here.

JOB: One of these days you're going to go too far....

(LENORE *tries to get the baseball bat.* BUTTERMAN *grabs* JOB *and leads him out.* LENA *grabs the bat before* LENORE.)

LENORE: Come on, Moms, it's too hot for this shit.

(LENORE *sits and begins snorting* BUTTERMAN's *cocaine.* BUTTERMAN *returns and looks at her for a beat.*)

BUTTERMAN: Hey, Lenore, that stuff costs money. Lighten up on my blow, unless you've got some cash.

LENORE: Got plenty of money. Sixty thousand to be exact.

(*Pause*)

BUTTERMAN: Aye...check it out, I ain't into games, you are fuckin' with your life here.

LENORE: No, I don't think so. Maybe I'm fuckin' with your life.... I wonder what those guineas will do when you turn up with no money.

BUTTERMAN: What the fuck are you talkin' about? We're talkin' about my money, and I want it now.

LENA: Don't mess with the Butterman, Moms.

LENORE: I ain't gonna mess with him, I'm gonna shit on him so those Italians he works for flush him down the toilet.

ACT ONE

BUTTERMAN: I don't work for nobody.

LENA: You know the Butterman is his own man, Moms.

LENORE: I know he's into them mobsters for a lot of money. Can't you see girl? He's just frontin' for them.

BUTTERMAN: I don't know what it is you're tryin' to run down here, but you'd better listen to me when I tell you....

LENORE: No, you listen, I told you to have your ass back here in fifteen minutes, but you took thirty.

BUTTERMAN: Don't play with my money.

LENORE: Your money? Check it out, you play with my daughter, so I'm gonna play with your balls.

LENA: I think you had too much to drink...too much blow.... Do you realize who you're messing with? Now just chill, and give Butterman his money....

LENORE: You know what?... I think you should go to bed.

LENA: I'm not going anywhere.

LENORE: This twenty-four-hour hard-on ain't gonna be around all night.

BUTTERMAN: Baby girl, me and your mother need to talk.

(LENA *goes into the bedroom.*)

LENORE: I don't like this shit. You got my daughter's nose... my son's nose. What kinda voodoo you runnin' on them?

BUTTERMAN: I simply have their respect.

LENORE: Respect? Hah! You must really have them fooled.

BUTTERMAN: I expect that kind of reaction out of the likes of you.

LENORE: The likes of me?... You jive-ass-lame-cokehead-Mafia-flunky-son-of-a-bitch... (*She looks upward.*) God, God, God, what is it with these people who think they are better than me?

BUTTERMAN: You know, I know...shit, everybody knows, if it weren't for Job and the welfare....

LENORE: Job is mine...the welfare money is mine....

BUTTERMAN: Bitch, nothin' is yours. You ain't never had nothin' of your own. That's why you tryin' to get Baby Girl to pull this boy's chain. What the fuck is yours in this world?... Twice a month you stand in line...your hands soaking from anticipation of food stamps and cash. Okay, okay...so you party the weekend into oblivion, but when you open your smoked-out, coked-out eyes to Monday morning, it's two more weeks of gasping for air before the next go-'round, courtesy of Public Assistance.... Yeah, barely enough air to keep you alive... But what can you do? You're a lifer. And Job? Light a match within ten feet of him and watch him become a human torch. Really now, how much blood do you think is in his alcohol?

LENORE: Look ahere, get up off my old man.

BUTTERMAN: Fuck that. Who the fuck you think you're talkin' to? Job is one useless old man.

LENORE: He bring a check in here every week. He's a better man than you'll ever be....

BUTTERMAN: He's nothin' but a alcoholic....

LENORE: Yeah, well...that alcoholic...that juice fiend...he picked me up when a dog wouldn't piss on me.... Used to see me every day...told me I was too good for walkin' the streets.... See, he snatched me from the pit. Beat the shit out of low-life like you and told him, "This is mine." That was balls...to come after me, love me, care for me, and take my shit. Don't go talking about what you don't know... Don't nobody mess with Job but me. I'll kill a nigger who fuck with Job.... Man feed me and my babies.

BUTTERMAN: I see more drinking than feeding.... See, I may not be with my babies, but I feed them. One day some youngblood may take me out, people will talk shit about me. Word. But they can't say the Butterman didn't take care of his. With his money... You? Well, obviously your life is fucked.

(Silence)

LENORE: Your life is better?

BUTTERMAN: My life is the serious. The death.

ACT ONE   41

LENORE: The only thing you're serious about is flunkying for those linguini-eatin' guineas in Sheepshead Bay.

(He laughs.)

BUTTERMAN: They are my partners.

LENORE: Be for real, those Sicilians don't have partnerships with niggers.

BUTTERMAN: But they do with ambitious black men.... Hey, how did I get into this? I don't have to prove a damn thing to you. Give me my money.

LENORE: I don't know what money you're talkin' about.

BUTTERMAN: Get up off my money. *(Long pause)* What do you want?

LENORE: Leave Lena alone.

BUTTERMAN: Why should I?

LENORE: Because I've got your money. I'm the only one who knows where it is. I ain't frontin' when I say you touch me you'll never see your money again.

(Pause)

BUTTERMAN: I can set her up like a queen. I can make it happen quick. I'll give her anything I can beg, borrow, or steal.

LENORE: Long-range, Butterman, long-range. She marries him and she'll be big time....

BUTTERMAN: Name a man, woman, or dog in C.I. who don't respect me.

LENORE: Fuck that rinky-dink shit. I'm talkin' the serious big time. Now I want you to stay away from her until she's married and pregnant.

BUTTERMAN: You don't understand.... Suppose...I...uhhh...uhhh...what if I married her?

LENORE: Are you jerking me or what? *(She looks at him.)* Is this the real deal?... Ain't this some shit. *(She laughs.)*

BUTTERMAN: You think it's funny? You that far gone, Lenore? 'Cause I'm the Butterman I'm not supposed to want anybody? What I work hard for? To come home to nothin'? Damn it I deserve a life too. I want to make Baby Girl that one person I can...I....

(LENORE laughs some more.)

BUTTERMAN: I just need to know that one person is on my side. But you can't even understand that. You're a real bitch.

LENORE: And you're a god-damned dog in heat. That slut-bitch of daughter of mine has got your nose wide open. The Butterman has a serious love-jones for my little girl.

BUTTERMAN: Her and that boy are from different worlds.

LENORE: Long as they get married in this world. Look ahere, are you gonna leave my daughter alone? 'Cause if you don't I'm sixty-thousand dollars richer.

BUTTERMAN: I'd kill you for my money.

LENORE: What the fuck is life? I don't give a fuck about life.

(She goes into the kitchen. A beat. She returns with the meat cleaver. BUTTERMAN backs up, but LENORE grabs him by the arm and hands the utensil to him.)

LENORE: Law of the street says you will kill my ass on G.P. so everybody know you don't play with the Butterman's cash.

BUTTERMAN: You got that right.

(LENORE bows to BUTTERMAN like a French aristocrat before her executioner. She crosses her hands behind her back, kneels, and places her head on the coffee table. BUTTERMAN stands over her with the meat cleaver. Long pause)

BUTTERMAN: Lenore...

LENORE: Is that the voice of an angel? Have I really made it to heaven?

(LENORE looks up at BUTTERMAN.)

BUTTERMAN: I'll leave her alone.

ACT ONE 43

LENORE: Ah, shit, I'm still in hell, face to face with a black demon.

BUTTERMAN: Fuck you.

LENORE: Oh, you will, you will.

(LENORE *goes to* BUTTERMAN. *She rubs her hand over his chest.* BUTTERMAN *grabs her by the wrist and pulls her hand off him.*)

BUTTERMAN: What's this?

(She begins to open his shirt. BUTTERMAN *removes her hand again.)*

LENORE: I've never heard tell of you refusing a little round of stroke and poke. Don't tell me now that I've got you you're nothin' but a myth.

BUTTERMAN: I have my pick of the litter, and I do my own picking.

LENORE: Yeah, well, you turn this bitch down and you'll be sixty thousand dollars in the hole. *(Pause)* First time I saw you...you were over on Surf Avenue selling Muslim newspapers. Let's see.... You were in a blue pin-striped suit with a white shirt and a red bowtie.... Had the nerve to be a gentleman.

BUTTERMAN: Yo, that wasn't me. You've got me mixed up with somebody else. The Butterman ain't never done some wack shit like that. *(He laughs.)*

LENORE: That was you nigger.

BUTTERMAN: The young man you're describing doesn't sound like a nigger to me. *(Pause)* You ought to know that there wasn't any niggers in the Nation of Islam. That was the point. No niggers. They got them while they were young...or young and after their first time in the joint.... They'd grab on to you in the joint, take a hold of your mind and soul, like that good blotter acid Reed been dibbin' and dabbin' in.... They'd take you on a trip all right.... A trip about yourself and who you are, and where you came from and where you were going. If you didn't know where you were going they'd point you there. It was about liftin' up yourself and everybody around you. It was about being a courteous gentleman, but it wasn't about turning your cheek. It was about protectin' yourself and your loved ones.... The brothers and sisters were so nice and polite to each other.... And if you liked an available lady you had to let your intentions be known, and if she thought you worthy she might give you the privilege of getting to know her, but only in a public situation...within the guidelines of whatever mosque she belonged to...and of course, with the approval of her father....

LENORE: Shit, then what happened to you?... Oh, yeah, Ruth Garrison pulled your ass off the corner.... Kept passin' you every day. You was just standin' there sellin' your papers...your nice little haircut.... Clean-shaven... But Ruthie could feel your eyes on her every time she walked by.... So she bet all of us that she could snatch you from that Muslim bag.... That she could turn your little lame square-ass out.... And she did it...she turned you out....

BUTTERMAN: Of course sometimes a brother would fall back to his old ways, or if he was young, and had never experienced life.... There would be a woman.... Not one of those beautiful sisters from the mosque...but one of them hot sisters with them tight-ass mini-skirts, them red halter tops on top of brown skin, wearin' them open-toed "fuck-me" shoes.... She was usually older, and she had a power over the boy that even Islam couldn't battle. And she'd take him and give him a little bit at a time.... It be so good...as soon as he'd dip himself in her he'd pop off...that hot...that good.... And she'd school him on how to make her feel good.... She'd keep him up all night.... And pretty soon he wasn't on his corner selling papers any more...or bean pies.... Yeah, he was interested in pie all right.... Her special hot, sweet, nookie pie...he was eatin' it all right.... That's the first thing she taught him.... And she taught him well. Being older and far more experienced she turned him on to freak scenes with other women. At first he hesitated... this wasn't the way it was supposed to be between a man and a woman. And she assured it was...how else was he supposed to learn how to please her correctly.... She said the same thing when she brought some dude into the bed.... And you knew in your gut that it was wrong....

ACT ONE   45

But you didn't have the power to leave. Did you? It was more than love...it was had-to-have-it fever. I...he...had to have it...no matter the cost or degradation of his soul. He couldn't get enough, and he was lasting longer...partially because of what she'd taught him, and partially because of the cocaine she'd stuffed up his nose.... And when the Mosque finally expelled him for his degenerate ways.... She had him. And she was pregnant.... And it was "time to do somethin' nigger".... And you talk about gettin' a job and she laughs a poor fool laugh. You'd better learn how to scramble...how to deal...how to gamble...how to pimp...how to run a scam...a kick-ass Murphy on some lame-ass sucker...how to kill...for a reason or just because you don't like a motherfucker.... It becomes easy, and you forget that you were something proud once...someone worthy of admiration, because you had it together...you were once someone worthy of being loved. *(Pause)* So you see, Lenore...that young man you're describing wasn't the Butterman, and he definitely wasn't a nigger.

LENORE: All that humpin' and bumpin' you were talkin' about got me horny. You want your money? Then you gonna have to gimme some of what this woman taught that boy. Now are we gonna get it on or are we just gonna let your partners turn you into meatballs?

BUTTERMAN: What about Lena?

LENORE: Still frontin' that respect shit?

BUTTERMAN: When I was younger I used to kill suckers for disrespecting me. Maybe I'm gettin' old.

LENORE: Yeah, well, kill me and you're comin' right behind me, 'cause you'll never find the money.... I'll go check on her.

(LENORE *goes to the bedroom area.* BUTTERMAN *goes to the dinette table and picks up the vial of cocaine and begins to snort, using the spoon on the top, five or six times before* LENORE *comes back.* LENORE *returns.*)

LENORE: She's dead to the world.

BUTTERMAN: I don't know, Lenore, she could wake up.

LENORE: I don't have to tell you how sound she sleeps.

BUTTERMAN: Okay, okay, let's us make this quick. *(He snorts more coke.)*

LENORE: Quick my ass. If you're quick on the trigger you ain't never gettin' your money back.

(He continues his snorting.)

BUTTERMAN: When I get through you ain't gonna be nothin' left for nobody.

(He closes up the vial, grabs her by the hand, and begins to lead her toward the bedroom area. She stops him.)

LENORE: Where do you think you're going?

BUTTERMAN: Your bedroom.

LENORE: What do you think this is? Who do you think I am?

BUTTERMAN: What are you yip-yappin' about? I thought you wanted to get down?

LENORE: Yeah, but not in my bed. Not in me and my old man's bed.

BUTTERMAN: Why not?

LENORE: That's me and my husband's bed. I got pregnant with my last child in that bed. Do you think I'd lay in that bed with you? Do you think I'd do that to my marriage?

BUTTERMAN: Fine. The kids' room...they're in camp....

LENORE: No way.

BUTTERMAN: Then where the hell are we supposed to do it?

(LENORE looks around, and then makes a grand gesture meaning they are to do it right there, in the living room. She sits on the couch. He follows.)

BUTTERMAN: You're a real freak, Lenore.

LENORE: It takes one to know one. Does Lena have some freak in her too? *(Pause)* Oh, don't get so uptight, I'm just teasing.

(BUTTERMAN kisses her. She pulls away abruptly.)

LENORE: I'm no school girl. I don't need nobody's tongue.

ACT ONE

(She kisses him on the neck, then bites him.)

BUTTERMAN: Not so rough, Baby.

LENORE: I like it rough. What are you a virgin?

BUTTERMAN: Just take it easy.

LENORE: Take it easy? I expect sixty-thousand dollars' worth of humping out of you.

BUTTERMAN: Just shut up.

LENORE: I'll shut up when I start feelin' somethin' besides your lap. *(She takes his hands and places them on her breasts.)* Squeeze... C'mon, like you mean it... What's the matter with you, Lame?

BUTTERMAN: You're blowin' my head.

LENORE: You're blowin' somethin' good.

BUTTERMAN: Okay, okay...let's just wait a minute....

LENORE: Well, I really didn't think I'd have to wait a second for the Butterman, the walkin' hard-on. *(She feels his lap.)* Not a sign of life.

BUTTERMAN: Christ.

LENORE: We're not here for no religious experience.

BUTTERMAN: What the hell are we doin' here?

LENORE: I'm beginning to wonder.

BUTTERMAN: Where's my coke?

(LENA enters in a houserobe. BUTTERMAN looks up at LENA. LENORE looks straight ahead.)

LENA: What is this?

LENORE: Nothing. Believe me when I tell you, absolutely nothing.

BUTTERMAN: I thought you said she was sleeping?

LENORE: You believe everything I tell you?

BUTTERMAN: This is a bad dream.

LENORE: You got that right, and you're the star.

(LENA *comes over and stands over them.*)

LENORE: Now, see, like I been telling you, the nigger ain't shit.

BUTTERMAN: Would you get up off me, Lenore?

(LENORE *does not move.* LENA *slaps the* BUTTERMAN. *Pause.* BUTTERMAN *grabs her and pulls her down to kiss him.* LENORE *remains on his lap.*)

LENORE: You think you can get him to come to life?

(*With* LENA *still kissing him, and* LENORE *on his lap, unnoticed,* REED *comes in. He takes in the scene. He tries to scream but nothing comes out. He grabs his own throat.* BUTTERMAN *sees* REED. *He stops kissing* LENA, *and pushes* LENORE. *He gets up and fixes his pants. Meanwhile* REED *is in a wild frenzy.* REED *rips off his own shirt.*)

LENORE: That fool is having a fit.

BUTTERMAN: Reed...

REED: So this is the real deal, huh, Butterman?

(BUTTERMAN *tries to touch him but* REED *recoils.*)

BUTTERMAN: It's me, partner....

REED: I'm in the peak of my trip and what do I walk into but the peak of reality? All the time we been together.... Man, you took me so many places in my mind...your... mind.... You prepared me for some heavy shit...some heavy shit. Don't worry about it...it ain't no big thang.... Just about gettin' a nut, right y'all? Butterman taught me the essence of that. It's just a mind thing 'cause when you got the bitch's head the body will follow. That's what my man the Butterman taught me. Bet you he didn't teach y'all that...'cause it's a secret, between men. Right, sweet Butterman? Between men!

BUTTERMAN: Reed, let me explain....

REED: You ain't gotta run nothin' down to me.... I've just experienced the whole thing in Technicolor.... Some MGM shit...like walkin' on the set of *The Wizard of Oz* when the Munchkins was gettin' down.... Little people just gettin' down.... I see the bad bitch, and bitch Toto, and the fuckin'

ACT ONE 49

Tin Man with the tin heart.... But where's the Good Witch?... Where the fuck is the Good Witch?... See, I ain't got no ruby slippers.... I can't get the fuck out of here without Glenda, the Good Witch.... Where the fuck are you!!! Please, I want to go home.

(REED *backs away, then closes his eyes and begins clicking his heels together.*)

LENORE: That boy is stuck on a trip he ain't never comin' down off of.

REED: There's no place like home...there's no place like home...there's no place like home...there's no place like home....

(BUTTERMAN *goes to* REED.)

BUTTERMAN: Calm down, my Man, you're having a bad trip. But the Butterman is here to get you through.

(REED *jumps on* BUTTERMAN *and tries to choke him. They wrestle and fall to the floor.* BUTTERMAN *is trying to hold* REED *down. But* REED, *with his acid peaking, is starting to get the best of* BUTTERMAN. LENORE *backs away from the action.*)

LENA: We've got to do somethin', Moms....

LENORE: Nigger, ain't my child...

(REED *is on top of* BUTTERMAN *now, getting the best of him.* LENA *comes over to help.* REED *punches her in the stomach. She buckles to the floor in pain.* LENORE *goes to her.* REED's *hands are around* BUTTERMAN's *throat.*)

LENORE: Reed, you're killing him.

(*After several beats,* BUTTERMAN *passes out.* REED *turns and rises and looks at* LENORE *and* LENA.)

REED: Moms... You tried to school me, but I didn't learn. I flunked.... I didn't know that at the bottom of the pit there was only darkness.... Is this why you wanted us around?... There's no place like home...no place home...except I don't have a home...so where am I to go. The Wizard? No luck, he's off to Kansas...some one-dog, no-nigger town.... So I'm stuck here in the haunted forest.... The Emerald City is dead...and the poppy fields have been fucking Napalmed by the wicked bitch's flying monkeys. Why'd you do that, Moms? I'm stuck here, and I ain't never goin' back...'cause of the moment you just gave me, dear old Moms. What's next? A Sunday picnic at the beach?

(LENORE *sees* REED *eyeing the meat cleaver on the kitchen table. Pause. They both race for the table.* REED *beats her to the cleaver.*)

LENORE: *(Backing away)* You stay away from me you black fuck.

(REED *draws closer to his mother. Quickly, she takes a chair from the dinette table and puts it between herself and* REED—*the way a lion tamer would tame a beast.*)

LENORE: Get back, get back or I'll ram this chair down your throat.

(REED *draws closer.*)

LENORE: Do you hear, Motherfucker?

REED: You fucked your son in so many ways.... That makes you a son-fucker.

(*He begins to laugh. First low, then hysterically. He cannot stop.* LENORE *starts to maneuver her way with the chair between herself and the laughing* REED. *He does not notice her, as he is caught up in his laughter. She drops the chair and runs off to the bedroom area, hopping over* LENA *and the* BUTTERMAN. *A door is heard slamming. It stuns* REED *out of his laughter. He looks around for* LENORE.)

REED: The cunning, black-hearted, slut-bitch of a whore mother.

(REED *runs to the bedroom area. The sound of a door being chopped is heard.* REED *is heard laughing. He comes out.*)

REED: What could death mean to her?

(*He goes over to* LENA. *She is out of breath, but still conscious. He puts the cleaver to her throat for a beat. Then he goes over to* BUTTERMAN, *who is still knocked out.*)

REED: So...I was fooled too.... You had me going, Brother.... I thought that not only could I understand your pain, but that I could feel your pain.... Man, we got into it...and I thought we shared bits of ourselves that nobody else could

ACT ONE 51

dig. You really had me going...had me thinking that there was something underneath the shit.... I was sure...the more and more we talked, that you would find the road back... back...back to your humanity...your truth.... And I'd be right there with you, Butterman.... We'd rise together like the phoenix...and it wouldn't be about hustlin' and gettin' over.... It would be about standin' tall...and we'd be so beautiful...so gleaming in the light with our pin- striped suits and our bow-ties...and everybody would know the word, and they would all fall in line. And now I can see, truly see, that the only thing beneath the shit...is shit.

(REED *goes off to the kitchen area, dropping the cleaver on the dinette table as he does. Cabinets are heard opening and shutting...pots rattling. Pause.* REED *comes out carrying a waste-paper basket. He places it on the table. Out of this basket he takes the bag of drugs that* BUTTERMAN *gave him in Scene Two. Then he pulls out the money that* BUTTERMAN *gave* LENORE. *He laughs, then pulls out matches.*)

REED: Nice hiding place, Moms.

(*He spreads the money out, dropping it all into the basket. He picks up the bottle of Dewar's and pours it in the basket over the money and drugs. He lights the whole book of matches and throws it into the basket. As the fire starts to rise,* BUTTERMAN *wakes up.*)

BUTTERMAN: What the hell are you doing with that fire?

(REED *smiles, then goes into the kitchen.* BUTTERMAN *gets up and goes over to the basket.*)

BUTTERMAN: Oh shit!

(*He tries to put out the fire, but can't.* BUTTERMAN *runs into the kitchen and returns with a pitcher of water which he pours into the basket. The fire dies, but* BUTTERMAN *knows it is too late. As he looks into the kitchen,* BUTTERMAN *picks up the cleaver from the table.*)

LENA: Butterman, don't hurt him.

(*She goes to stop* BUTTERMAN. *Just as he pushes her out of the way, a scream is heard from the kitchen.* BUTTERMAN *takes a step forward and takes a look in the kitchen. He looks like he is about to become sick from what he sees. He steps back and drops the cleaver.* LENA *looks puzzled, but afraid to see for herself.* LENORE *comes out.)*

LENORE: What's that fool done now?

BUTTERMAN: His eyes...he gouged his eyes out...he gouged his damn eyes out.

*(*REED *is heard screaming again, then an ominous moan.* LENA *tries to go into the kitchen, but* BUTTERMAN *holds her back. Knocking is heard at the door. More moaning from the kitchen is heard.* LENORE *is backing away, going to answer the door.* REED *comes to the entrance to the kitchen. His eyes are bleeding—there is a fork in each hand. He stands there as* LENORE *returns with* CODY, *who is still in his ape suit.* REED *stumbles into the living room, dropping the forks, and then falling to the floor and covering his bloody eyes.* BUTTERMAN *runs to the kitchen.* LENORE *starts to go to him, but then can't bear it.* LENA *goes to comfort* REED.*)*

LENA: I'm here, Reed.

*(*REED *pushes her away.* CODY *goes to him.* LENORE *goes to the window.)*

LENORE: Job! Job!

*(*BUTTERMAN *returns with a towel and places it over* REED's *eyes.* REED *calms down as he feels* CODY's *ape suit.)*

REED: Cody?

CODY: What the hell happened?

REED: The real deal, Cody, the real deal...

LENORE: Job, please...Job...

(Lights fade.)

END OF ACT ONE

ACT TWO
Prologue

(In the dark, thunder. Lightning is seen flashing through the upstage windows, and low rumbling thunder throughout "Reed's Rap". Lights up on REED. *He wears shades and carries a blind man's cane. Rap music begins to play.)*

REED: Gimme that kick, gimme that kick!
Ya baby's a trick, ya baby's a trick!
KICK IT!

(Lights up behind LENA *and the* APE *standing behind the couch.* LENA *is in a sexy robe. She is leaning on the back of the couch, her hands braced on the back of the couch. The* APE *is making love to her from behind as* REED *raps.)*

REED: Get up off the hope
Abandon all your dreams
This here is the dope
The Beast is on the scene
He's a big-time liar
Sweet talk you to death
Throw you in the fire
Forget about the rest
You can't cut no deal
'Cause you're lost in smoke
Better get real
'Cause you've lost all hope

You can't trick me, huh
In the middle of a groove
I may be blind
But I see all the moves

Watch out, Suckas
For the kick in the butt
From them low-life niggas
Layin' in the cut
Now they'll stomp you down
Or they'll jive you around
You'll think you're in bliss
But you're nuthin' but a clown

LENA & APE: You got me workin'...

REED: Gimme that kick,
Gimme that kick,

LENA & APE: I'm a misplaced soul...

REED: Gimme that kick,
Gimme that kick,

LENA & APE: You got me jerkin'

REED: Gimme that kick,
Gimme that kick,

LENA & APE: Gonna lose control

REED: Gimme that kick!

(LENA *and the* APE *collapse in orgasmic frenzy behind the couch.*)

REED: You don't think about peace
Sleepin' with the beast
Now don't you dare ask me
Who the hell he be
Because you and I know
Who's runnin' the show
So forget your humanity
Feast with insanity
In this world of profanity
There's peace in calamity
Prepare yourself
And keep your mind intact
Beware of the fact
That he is the "Big Mac"

'Cause you're bound
For the seductive

ACT TWO

Torturous hell
The unproductive
Deep dark well
The destructive
Listen what I tell...

THE ABYSS!

(Blackout)

Scene One

(One month later. The Fourth of July. Before the lights come up, the Wonder Wheel is seen turning. Fireworks are heard going off in the distance. As the lights come up, CODY and LENA are making love. As in the Prologue, with the APE, LENA is being made love to from behind by CODY. They are lit mostly by the lightning. They climax with the sound of thunder. They rest for a beat, then CODY moves away in the dark of the house, finding his underwear and putting them on. He goes to lay on the couch. LENA is still leaning against the couch. Finally, she pulls down the back of her robe, then comes around to the front of the couch to be with CODY. The lights come fully up to reveal CODY in a pair of boxer shorts covered with valentine hearts. CODY opens her robe and begins kissing her stomach. She picks up a joint from the coffee table and lights it. Then she picks up a can of Miller beer and begins sipping from it.)

LENA: Was it good, Baby?

CODY: Mmmm hmmmmm.

LENA: We'll go another round after I smoke this joint.

(She tries to pass him the joint.)

LENA: It'll make you horny again.

CODY: Looking at you makes me horny again.

(She pulls him to her and starts licking his chest.)

LENA: I like the sound of that. *(She feels his crotch.)* The feel of that too.

(CODY pulls away nervously.)

LENA: What's wrong with you?

CODY: Shouldn't they be coming in from the beach soon?

LENA: It's the Fourth of July, these project picnics last sometimes 'til two or three in the morning. It ain't even midnight yet.

(Still, CODY looks nervous. He goes to look out the window. As she deeply inhales her joint, LENA takes a long look at CODY.)

LENA: Let me ask you something, Cody.

CODY: Yeah?

LENA: Do you really want me?

CODY: After making love like this...all day...deep into the night.... This last month has been just what we needed.

LENA: What the fuck are you sayin'?...

CODY: I love you.

(LENA laughs.)

LENA: Yeah, Cody, but do you want me?

CODY: Is there a point here?

LENA: Oh, yeah. There's a point.... Something's got to give. You need to either start working on your mother, or get a job.

CODY: I need a job...you're right...something to work around my acting classes.

LENA: You still putting this acting shit before me.

CODY: What do you mean "Acting shit"? You know this is what I want to do. Since we were kids. Now, all of sudden, the only thing I ever wanted to do is shit? It's what I love.

LENA: Yeah, well, next time you get hard...you go stick it in some acting. You want me? Time to get a job, Nigger.

CODY: That's what this place has done to you? Job? Lena, I don't want a job, I want a career.

LENA: Career? Acting? We're gonna line our stomachs with the hope that you're talented?

ACT TWO 57

(She laughs as she picks up the scotch from the table and pours herself a drink.)

LENA: Let me tell you something, if we're going to be together, I don't want to be scufflin'. I don't want to be worried about the rent, or if my kid has food. You talking about us being together? Get on the good foot. You better get with it, Cody. It's time to pick up your marbles and throw them away. Grow up! See, your mother never told you that you were a nigger like everybody else. Acting? Pure white boy shit.... They've got all the time in the world to fantasize about "careers", but Cody, you're a nigger, and no self-respecting nigger is fucking around in acting classes or college.... He's out there with a job, or a hustle, or both.

CODY: Yeah, sure. Why not? I could sell poison to people just like the Butterman.

LENA: You haven't got the balls.

CODY: No shit. I don't want those kind of balls.

LENA: Why you always tryin' to dis' the Butterman?

CODY: The word is disrespect.

LENA: Just answer my fucking question!

CODY: The answer is obvious.

LENA: It sure is. *(She sips her drink knowingly.)* Well, you always did hate your daddy.

CODY: You don't know what you're talking about....

LENA: Especially what he was.

CODY: What he was was an educated man.

LENA: A hustler is a hustler. In his heart of hearts that's what your daddy was. Shit, he was no different than the Butterman.

(CODY raises his hand to slap her.)

LENA: Go ahead, slap the living shit out of me if I'm lyin'.

(CODY puts his hand to his side.)

LENA: And silence is golden. You know what I'm talking about. Men like the Butterman...your father, the men with big balls? They get over like fat rats. Sure, Butterman is probably dead now, it's been over a month since he disappeared, but when he was alive he was the man. And I'll bet you he died like a man.

CODY: Let me tell you something, my father was nothing like the Butterman, that slithering, slimey, slickster who got your brother so freaked out he put his own eyes out.

(LENA *throws her drink in* CODY's *face. She then pours herself another drink.*)

(Pause)

CODY: You're not my Lena. You're not the little girl who used to help my mother in the garden.... The girl who gave herself to me...only me...and then cried because she thought making love was a sin.

(Pause)

(She takes a step toward him. She opens her robe.)

(Pause)

(He goes to her and kisses her on the lips. Then he kisses her on the neck. He then drops to his knees and begins to kiss her crotch area.)

LENA: Do you want it, Baby?...

CODY: Yes...yes...

(She moves away from him abruptly and closes her robe.)

LENA: See, I'm my Lena. *(Tossing her head back as she downs her drink)* You're mumbling about some little girl...a ghost. I'm my Lena, a hot, horny, hungry woman. Now which one do you want? *(Pause)* Hey, I've got no time for dream merchants...and neither does your baby. *(Pause)* You don't want to do the do? No problem. This girl knows when a lame is frontin'. It's time to step off. I got no problem with flushing your little bastard down the toilet. I'm not gonna carry around your baby without some gold on my finger, without feeling you up against me every night. I don't know what you think the fuck this is, but, get this clear, I am not my mother.

(Silence)

ACT TWO

CODY: This is my baby?

LENA: I don't fuckin' believe you. I've loved you since before I knew what love was, and you could fix your lips to ask me that? Don't worry about it. I'll take care of everything.

(She moves away from him to the other side of the room. After a beat, he goes to her and embraces her from behind.)

CODY: It's going to be okay, Lena. We'll work it out. We'll take care of our baby.

(She turns to him.)

CODY: The first thing we've got to do is get you out of Coney Island.

LENA: I don't want to go back to Long Island....

CODY: We can move someplace else. Anywhere you want.... I was telling Reed about California....

LENA: California?

CODY: Yeah, me, you, Reed, and the baby can start over there.

LENA: On what?

CODY: Have a little faith, Lena. I just don't want our kid born here. We're better than this. We did not come from this, Lena. I don't want to live here, and you don't either.... Not really. We're going to have a child.... We can't play with its future.... I can't imagine you having our baby in Coney Island Hospital.... I can't see us riding him up a pissy elevator on his first day home. That's death. Don't misunderstand me, no disrespect to your mother, but we don't want this for our kids. What we want is the best, you used to want the best, but now you've come here and your wants and needs have become distorted. You think that to love your mother you have to embrace everything around her. I encourage you to embrace her, but don't embrace Coney Island.

LENA: There's nothing wrong with C.I. I like it here. When we were growing up I always felt like I was acting like something I wasn't. I could never put it into those words, but it always seemed to me that we always had to act a certain way. My aunt was always on me and Reed not to act like "niggers". It was always, "We don't want them people in the neighborhood, or at the school, thinking you're no-account niggers". See, we was raised to worry about what other people think of us. That's why I like Coney Island, I don't got to be nobody but who I am.

CODY: When I get you out of here, you'll remember how it was. I don't want this for us.

LENA: How about what I want for us? Ain't nothing wrong with C.I., at least our kids will know who they are.

CODY: We are not from this.

LENA: I am. And if you look real hard you'll see that you are too.

(There is a knock at the door. LENA goes to answer it. CODY pours himself a drink. LENA returns with a woman—in fact, it's the BUTTERMAN in drag. He wears a long black shoulder-length wig, a conservative business suit which consists of a grey skirt and jacket, a pink blouse with a brooch on the top button, pocketbook, and earrings. He still wears shades, but they are of a feminine style. On his feet are a pair of Nike running shoes, and he is wearing pink footsies that have pom poms hanging over the back of the shoes. Thinking BUTTERMAN a woman, CODY ducks behind the couch. LENA is totally dazed by this BUTTERMAN in drag.)

CODY: Why didn't you tell me you were bringing in a lady?

LENA: This is no lady, this is the Butterman.

(CODY slowly rises from behind the couch. Like LENA, he just stares at the BUTTERMAN.)

BUTTERMAN: This house smells like sex.

(BUTTERMAN is uncomfortable at their staring. After a beat, he moves to the window and looks out. They both go over to him, continuing to stare.)

BUTTERMAN: What the hell y'all lookin' at?

(He goes over to the kitchen table and pours himself a drink. CODY gulps down his own drink. He then takes the bottle and

ACT TWO 61

pours himself another. LENA *takes an unlit joint out of the ashtray, lights it, and then takes a long drag.* CODY *gets closer to* BUTTERMAN. CODY *begins to laugh and, after a beat,* LENA *joins him.)*

BUTTERMAN: Y'all think I'm a joke or somethin'?

CODY: Hey, Butterman, you've got one sweet ass.

(BUTTERMAN *looks at the laughing* LENA. *He takes a sip of his drink and moves downstage.* CODY *follows.)*

CODY: So, we're dressing incognegro these days?

BUTTERMAN: Hey, you heart-underwear-wearing motherfucker, kiss my black ass.

CODY: My, my, my...in that tight-ass skirt you're wearing, I just might.

BUTTERMAN: Yo, step off. *(He goes to* LENA.*)* Where's your mother?

LENA: On the boardwalk.

BUTTERMAN: When is she coming back?

(LENA *shrugs.)*

BUTTERMAN: I need...I really need to see her....

LENA: Go look for her on the boardwalk....

BUTTERMAN: The ocean...I don't go nowhere near the ocean.... That bitch will suck you up in a minute. It will suck you then spit you back out. I know the ocean.... Made my baby girls by the ocean...under the boardwalk...

CODY: Sounds romantic...

BUTTERMAN: Romantic? Ain't no such sandwich.... See, that's what they want you to believe.... That woman...that Ruth, took me down there, all the time, in the deep of the night...took me down there...turned me out by the roar of the midnight sea-bitch.... That's where she worked the shit on me.... I didn't figure it out 'til much later.... You be ridin' your baby's tide...and she becomes one with it.... Don't ever make love by the ocean, Boy...'cause when the woman whisper in your ear it's like that sound you hear in the sea shells...and then there's that roar...that ocean...your body gets to shakin'...and the next thing you know, every bit of juice in your body is in the ocean.... She done beckoned it up...done willed it out of you.... *(Pause)* I was sucked in... whole bunch of times...I loved getting sucked in.... And so I don't go anywhere near that deadly bitch. *(Pause)* Lena, I've got to lay for your moms.

(LENA *turns away from him.*)

BUTTERMAN: Come on, Baby Girl, don't dis' me like that.

(She turns on him.)

LENA: You deserve to be dis'ed. Bogus three-dollar-bill nigger.... Sal and Vito are gonna serve your ass on a silver platter.

BUTTERMAN: They've been here?

LENA: Several times. But then the last couple of weeks they stopped coming.... So we all thought you were dead.

BUTTERMAN: You should be glad that I'm not.

LENA: As far as I'm concerned, the Butterman is dead. The Butterman I know sure wouldn't run around hiding in a dress. The Butterman I know...he would have laid in the cut and caught his enemy with his pants down...would have hung them by their balls with spaghetti.... You're too weak to be the Butterman. I don't know what you did with him, but you're not him.... You let us all down.

(BUTTERMAN *starts to touch her cheek, but she avoids him.*)

BUTTERMAN: Who the fuck did you think I was?

LENA: I thought you were somebody whose strings weren't being pulled...but you're just like the rest of these nigger men.

BUTTERMAN: Yeah, well, it bees that way sometimes. Get used to being let down. It's the way of the world, Baby Girl.

(BUTTERMAN *finishes his drink.* CODY *takes* LENA *gently by the hand and pulls her to him.*)

CODY: Lena...I'll never let you down...if you marry me.

LENA: Cody, this is not the time...there's too much to talk about....

ACT TWO

CODY: I can't think of a better time...or a better witness. Don't you want to?

LENA: What about your acting, Cody?... You can't have a family and pursue such foolishness. I don't think that's clear to you...that you have to make a choice.... Which do you love more.... If you want me...it's got to be the real deal. I don't want you standing here and saying you're going to give up something...and you don't mean it.

CODY: All I know is I want to be with you. I don't want nothing else. I'm going to set things up. Yeah, I'll sacrifice for you and our baby.

(BUTTERMAN *gives a startled look.*)

BUTTERMAN: You're just killing yourself, Boy.

LENA: If I'm your heart's desire, then I'm yours.

BUTTERMAN: You're pregnant?

LENA: Why? Is it supposed to mean something to you?

(Pause)

(BUTTERMAN *looks the two of them over.*)

BUTTERMAN: Not a god-damned thing, Baby.

(BUTTERMAN *goes to the dinette table. He picks up the deck of cards and begins to play solitaire. Low rumbling of thunder is heard.* LENA *and* CODY *embrace and kiss.* JOB *enters, carrying a bag of charcoal and the bottom part of a grill. He looks at the* BUTTERMAN *in drag and then back at the couple.*)

(Pause)

JOB: What kind of freak show is this?

(CODY *and* LENA *stop kissing.*)

JOB: This house smells like sex. What the hell do you think they have bedrooms for? Have some respect for my house, Nigger.

(CODY *runs quickly to the bedroom area.* JOB *stares at* LENA *She rolls her eyes, picks up the Kool cigarettes from the coffee table, lights one, and sits.* JOB *goes over to the* BUTTERMAN.*)

JOB: Who the hell are you, Lady?

BUTTERMAN: Don't fuck with me, Job, I'm not in the mood.

(JOB *looks closer.*)

(*Pause*)

(*He goes nose to nose with* BUTTERMAN.)

(*Pause*)

(JOB *breaks into laughter.*)

JOB: Damn, Butterman, I was just about to ask you for a piece of ass. (*He pours himself a drink.*) So it's true? Don Corleone really does have you on the run.

BUTTERMAN: Just shut your alcoholic mouth.

(*Pause*)

(JOB *takes a big swig of his drink.*)

JOB: Check this shit out, you don't tell me what to do. I'm the man of this house. You ain't got no rulin' rights here.... I know you can kick my ass, but if you mess with me, where I rule, well...we're going to be two rumbling cats.

(BUTTERMAN *laughs.*)

(*Thunder grows louder.*)

BUTTERMAN: You're one crazy old dude.

JOB: Damn right.... Want to get down on some cards?

BUTTERMAN: Nah, nah, maybe later.... Check it out, I've got some rap for Lenore.

JOB: Her and Reed are right behind me. (*Thunder. He goes to the window.*) They'd better hurry up or they'll wet.

(CODY *returns, fully dressed.* JOB *turns and sees him. He goes over to* CODY, *right in his face. He stares.*)

JOB: Dummy, dummy, dummy...

LENA: Take your drunk ass to sleep, Job.

JOB: Didn't you just hear me tellin' somebody about messin' with me in my own house? (*He grabs* CODY *by the collar.*) You are a dead man!

(He releases CODY, *gulps down his drink, and then picks up his charcoal and grill, and goes to the bedroom area. When he's gone,* CODY *laughs.)*

CODY: Your stepfather is one bizarre guy.

BUTTERMAN: Well, you should dig yourself.... *(Mocking)* "I mean, gee golly willikers, gosh dang, you're a pretty bizarre guy too."

CODY: Very funny. But who's sitting at the table looking like a bitch.

LENA: Cody!

CODY: Your shit is tired, Butterman, and everybody is tired of you.

BUTTERMAN: You think you can judge me? If them guineas were after you you'da been dead.

CODY: Just go away Butterman, go far away...

BUTTERMAN: Who the fuck you tellin' to go away?...

LENA: Whoever it is, it sure ain't the Butterman.

*(*BUTTERMAN *tries to say something to her.)*

LENA: Cody's right...I wish you'd disappear.

*(*LENORE *enters with* REED. REED *has dark glasses on to cover his mutilated eyes. He also has a cane. He carries a beach bag that is stuffed with blankets. A bottle of lighter fluid can be seen sticking out of the bag.* LENORE *is carrying a cooler, and the top of the grill that* JOB *was carrying.)*

LENORE: This house smells like...like...dead fish. *(She looks at* BUTTERMAN.*)* Ain't this some shit? The Butterman in drag.

REED: *(Singing)* Buttery, buttery, buttery, spreads sooo smooth...

LENORE: Shut the fuck up!

LENA: He can't help it, Moms.

LENORE: You can believe that shit if you want to.

*(*REED *puts down the beach bag, makes his way over to the TV, turns it on low, then sits on the floor.)*

LENORE: He got good sense.

(LENORE *looks at* BUTTERMAN *and giggles.*)

BUTTERMAN: I ain't got time for your shit.

LENORE: You got time to die, Nigger? 'Cause, see, I just ran into the linguini boys in the lobby.

BUTTERMAN: You ran into Sal and Vito in the lobby?

LENORE: Yeah, and dig this, get the fuck out of my house!

BUTTERMAN: You would do that to me?

LENORE: If they knew you were up here what would they do to me? You're putting my family at risk.

BUTTERMAN: You've got to let me crash here.

LENORE: I don't got to let you do anything but die.

BUTTERMAN: They'll kill me.

LENORE: Kill them...you're the Butterman.

BUTTERMAN: If I kill them I'm in worse trouble.

LENA: You always told me and Reed to face the enemy head on and intimidate them into disappearing.

CODY: Gee, Butterman, you're a regular ghetto guru.

LENA: You ain't shit.

BUTTERMAN: Hey, Baby Girl, you're not the same innocent little girl who came here a year ago, but I still love you, even though I know you ain't shit.

LENA: You're the one running from the white boys like a...a...a....

CODY: Pussy.

BUTTERMAN: You just beggin' me to kill you, ain't you, Boy?

REED: *(Singing)* Spreads like butter...smooth and creamy.... Right, Moms, right, Sis? There's nothing like wholesome butter.

CODY: See what you've done to him?

BUTTERMAN: Reed is like a brother to me.

ACT TWO 67

CODY: What does that matter considering that you'd sell your mother for a line of coke? The thought of you should make all of C.I. sick. You're a big part of what makes this world sick. I tried to warn Reed. I tried to make him see the light.

BUTTERMAN: You little self-righteous, preppie, snot-nosed bitch... I told you before don't be judgin' the Butterman. You gonna stand around and judge something you can't even comprehend? Brother, I have seen the light and I can tell you that it's bullshit. Ain't nothing to this whole thing.... You believe in something and I assure you someone is gonna burst it for you. Gonna tell me about how I make the world sick? Death look us all in the face the same way.... Don't matter what you've done. He teases you with that light, yeah, Motherfucker, you go towards that light...and you hear that music, sound like a Coltrane solo.... Maybe death play "Naima" for you, but you be thinkin' it's 'Trane, yeah...and you go toward what you think is the light...what you think is big John playin'...shit.... But it ain't 'Trane, hell the-fuck-no! Death picked that tune right out of your memory, like maybe that was playin' the night you went to your senior prom. So it's all in your head, 'cause Coltrane is in the abyss. You ain't gonna see him at the end of that light, 'cause at the end of the light is that black-robed son of a bitch holding a flashlight. And you look around for a minute and he turns that flashlight off.... And there ain't shit, 'cause see that's what nonexistence in the abyss is.

REED: Follow the yellow brick road! Follow the yellow brick road!

BUTTERMAN: So don't be judgin' me...don't be talkin' about showin' Reed the light.... I been to that edge.... I had the faith and I saw there was nothing there.

LENORE: And they say Reed is stuck on a trip and is never coming down. What the hell you been shootin', snortin, and smoking this last month?

BUTTERMAN: Memories.

CODY: Can't you all see that he's trying to get our sympathy? Moms, you should throw this phony out.

(BUTTERMAN *takes a step toward* CODY. CODY *takes a step back toward the window.*)

BUTTERMAN: You think you a man? Then come on with it, Bitch! I've grown tired of hearing you sell woof tickets.

CODY: You feeling froggy? You ready to leap?

BUTTERMAN: I'm gonna do you like we used to do lames in the joint. I'm gonna whip your ass, and then I'm gonna fuck you. Then I'm gonna run your ass back to Long Island. One day, when you become a man, you'll thank me for it.

(*It begins to rain hard.* CODY *takes another step back.* BUTTERMAN *pulls a switchblade from his bra.*)

CODY: Wait a minute, that's not fair.

BUTTERMAN: You think I got where I'm at today by being fair?

LENA: Do something, Moms.

LENORE: Butterman, you put that knife away right now. You hear me? Don't you ignore me.

(*She pushes him.*)

BUTTERMAN: Step off, Lenore.

LENORE: You keep fuckin' around and I'm gonna step off into your shit. Now you want to cut somebody, cut those guineas in the lobby since you feelin' brave.... Do you hear me, you limp-dick, wimp-bitch, faggot?

BUTTERMAN: Who you callin' a faggot?

LENORE: The motherfucker standing in front of me with a dress on. (*Pause*) Yeah, I know about you....

BUTTERMAN: What are you mumblin' about?...

LENORE: I ain't mumblin' jack-shit. I'm sayin' it loud. That's right, I called you a faggot! Shit, Ruth Garrison told me all about it. She had you in bed with another woman...and she had you in bed with another man...when she was breaking

ACT TWO 69

you in.... She used to brag about the things she could make her little Muslim boy do....

BUTTERMAN: So what? We both fucked her.

LENORE: And then he fucked you.

BUTTERMAN: What the fuck you say?

LENORE: Then he screwed you while you was doin' Ruth.

(BUTTERMAN *cuts* LENORE *on the side of her face.* LENORE *grabs the wound.*)

BUTTERMAN: You don't get in my face talkin' bullshit lies. You know better than that.

(LENA *grabs her mother.*)

LENA: Did he slice you deep?

BUTTERMAN: Quick and deep.

(LENORE *looks at the blood on her hand. She runs into the bedroom area.* LENA *follows.*)

CODY: You are an animal.

BUTTERMAN: *(Laughing)* No shit, Sherlock. Word! I am a lion. Fuck like a lion. Slaughter like a lion...and I guaran-fuckin'-tee ya I'll die like one. See you, you're a pussy.... You get fucked and you bleed. You'll die in your own blood as your butcher stands over you holding the balls you never had. That's why you can never have Lena...you have no manhood. If you did I would take it. But you can't take what was never there.

(CODY *charges* BUTTERMAN *as* LENORE, JOB, *and* LENA *enter.* LENORE *has a bat in hand.*)

JOB: Don't worry, Babes, I'll put foot in his ass.

(BUTTERMAN *pushes* CODY *off.* CODY *stands near the window.*)

BUTTERMAN: Time to pay them woof tickets, Boy.

(BUTTERMAN *charges* CODY. CODY *grabs him by the head with one hand, and by the hand with the switchblade.* BUTTERMAN *trips and falls out the window. As he does, Miles Davis' "'Round Midnight" begins playing.*)

(Silence)

(When CODY turns around he has BUTTERMAN's shades in one hand and his switchblade in the other. The music lowers slowly. They all look at CODY.)

CODY: I didn't mean it.... I didn't mean it to happen.... I was just.... I...I wasn't trying to kill him.... Really, I wasn't... trying....

LENORE: Nigger sliced up my face. Fuck him!

(CODY sits on the floor, his back up against the wall. LENA comes over to him. She stands over him, not really knowing quite what to do or say. She leaves CODY, and goes to look out the window. After a beat she goes back and sits on the floor with CODY.)

LENA: I'm glad it wasn't you.

CODY: It could have been me.

LENA: But it wasn't. *(Pause)* It wasn't the father of my child.

(JOB goes to the window and stares out.)

JOB: Eleven floors, damn!...

(REED takes a cigarette from his shirt pocket and places it in his mouth.)

JOB: Well, at least he's out of this shit. *(He begins to sob softly.)*

LENORE: That black spasm cut my face. Don't y'all dare waste a tear on him.

(REED is trying to light his cigarette. It is not lighting properly because he has the wrong end. LENA notices and goes over to him. She turns it around and lights it for him. He inhales.)

REED: Ahhh, the taste that refreshes. Thank you.

LENA: You're welcome. *(Pause)* Reed?

REED: *(Singing)* Thank you very much...thank you very much...I want to thank you very much....

LENA: The Butterman is dead....

REED: Humpty Dumpty sat on the wall
Humpty Dumpty had a great fall
All the King's horses

ACT TWO 71

And all the King's men
Couldn't put Humpty
Back together again....

LENORE: If the nigger don't really know what's going down, then why waste your breath on him?

(LENA *hugs* REED. *He does not respond.* CODY *is still sitting on the floor, staring at* BUTTERMAN's *switchblade and glasses.* LENORE *wipes her face and looks at the blood. She looks at* JOB. *He does not respond. Pause. She exits.* JOB *goes and sits at the dinette table.* LENA *goes back to* CODY.)

(*A scream is heard from the bedroom.*)

LENA: I guess she saw how deep it was.

JOB: She's been cut deeper than that.

LENA: But not on her face.

JOB: A cut is a cut.

(CODY *is literally shaking.* LENA *puts her arms around him.* LENORE *returns with a large gauze bandage on her face.*)

CODY: I guess...I guess we should call the police.

LENORE: What the hell for?

CODY: I just...just...killed the Butterman....

(LENORE *gives him a strange look.*)

CODY: It's murder....

LENORE: What's with this Perry Mason shit? Boy, this is Coney Island...see no evil, speak no evil....

CODY: It's better to turn yourself in.... They'll come...they'll investigate....

LENORE: White people don't investigate dead niggers...they ship 'em to potter's field. Listen here, this is not your fault. The Butterman fucked with you and he got fucked. Who would have thought you had the balls to stand up to the Butterman? It took big balls, Cody.

JOB: *(Distant)* Big balls...

(LENA *goes over to the table and pours herself a big drink.*)

LENORE: You all right, Girl?

LENA: Sure... *(Pause)* It's just that...I never knew anybody that died before.

LENORE: Everybody knows somebody that died....

LENA: I know people who've died, but I haven't *known* someone who has died.... I don't...I don't know how I'm supposed to feel about it...I don't know how I feel....

LENORE: You'll get used to it.... I done known a whole bunch of people that died...and, a lot of 'em, shit, I was glad they died....

LENA: Poor William...he didn't deserve to die like that....

LENORE: Poor who?

LENA: William Carter...that's the Butterman....

LENORE: *(Laughs)* No shit? I didn't know that. Nigger always had a moniker long as I know him.... Even when he was a young Muslim...first it was Billy X, then it was Mustafa Hakeem....

LENA: Who's gonna tell his daughters?...

JOB: They'll hear the drums, baby....

(REED *begins beating the top of the television like a conga player.*)

LENA: Death is...fucked up....

(LENORE *becomes irritated by* REED's *drumming. She goes over to him and slaps his hands.* REED *stops.*)

LENORE: Just praise the Lord that it ain't you...or your old man. *(She looks at* CODY.) Look at him.... Ain't he somethin'.... Right before our eyes.... Look at his face... he didn't used to look like that.... That's a man, Baby... that just-off-his-momma's left-titty-look is off his face.... He got that look....

CODY: Look?...

LENORE: It's all over your face....

CODY: It?

(CODY *gets up and starts toward the bedroom area.*)

ACT TWO 73

LENA: Where are you going, Cody?

CODY: To the bathroom to look in the mirror. *(He leaves.)*

(LENORE goes over and sits on the couch. She picks up a bag of reefer from the table, then some rolling papers. She begins rolling a joint. LENA looks at her. She starts to go to her mother, but then thinks better of it.)

(CODY is heard vomiting in the bathroom.)

(LENORE looks off toward the bathroom.)

LENORE: Y'all will learn to line your stomachs against death.... She's a greedy bitch, and the best thing to do with a greedy bitch is to ignore her, and make sure she don't eat you....

(LENA goes over to JOB, who is looking out the window. LENORE continues rolling her joint. The toilet is heard flushing.)

(LENA looks out the window.)

LENORE: Everybody get uptight 'bout death.... Shit, Butterman got it like I want it...to the quick....

(LENA looks at JOB. LENORE lights her joint and sits back on the couch. She is oblivous to LENA and JOB at the window.)

(LENA looks at JOB. A beat. They embrace. LENORE inhales her joint.)

(CODY comes in from the bathroom. They all turn and look at him. LENA goes to him and hugs him.)

LENA: I'm glad it wasn't you, Cody.

(CODY gives a strange look.)

LENORE: You damn right about that, Lena. When are you going to marry this boy?

LENA: He asked me right in front of the Butterman.

LENORE: Say what?... I told y'all this boy had big balls. *(She goes to them and hugs them both.)* Congratulations! You hear that, Job? My baby is going to get married.

(JOB is gazing out the window.)

JOB: I've got nothing to wear to the funeral.

LENORE: Fuck a funeral!... We're talking about a wedding.

(Sirens are heard.)

JOB: It's the ambulance...and the cops....

LENORE: Ambulance? Talk about a waste of money. Just get a big Hefty bag, scrape the son of a bitch up, and set him out to be picked up with the rest of the garbage.

LENA: You think they may come up and check?

LENORE: No way.... But maybe we should go down and mingle with the crowd.... Act shocked.... You think you can do that?

LENA: I can deal with it, Moms. I gotta get dressed first....

LENORE: Come on, Job, let's go downstairs and try to look dumb.

LENA: What about Cody?

(CODY goes and sits on the couch. He is in a daze.)

(LENORE pours CODY another drink.)

LENORE: Here, Baby.

(LENA goes off to the bedroom area. LENORE relights her joint which has gone out. She inhales, holds it for a beat, then exhales. She looks at CODY for a second, then she turns the lit end of the joint into her mouth, moves her face closer to CODY, puts the other end of the joint into CODY's mouth and blows smoke, giving him what is called a "shotgun". He inhales it deeply. She sits back on the couch and watches him as he holds the smoke in.)

(LENA returns, dressed in shorts and halter top.)

LENA: I'm ready, Moms.

LENORE: Let's go, Job.

(They leave. CODY finally exhales the smoke. He gets up and looks out the window. He becomes more shaken at what he sees down below. He goes back to the couch and takes a gulp of his drink. REED turns up the TV with the remote control. CODY looks downstage at REED.)

(Pause)

ACT TWO 75

(The sound of a car chase comes over the television. CODY *goes over and turns it down.)*

CODY: So what are you listening to?

REED: Get the fuck out of Dodge. Word up!

CODY: I can't believe that you'll never get back to normal.

REED: *(Singing)* Get back, get back, get back to your Long Island home.

(Pause)

CODY: Reed?... Nah, it's just me wishing you were back.... I wonder what you'd say if you knew I killed the Butterman? This place...it's starting to scare me....

REED: Splitsville!

CODY: ...but Lena wants to stay....

REED: Then fuck the bitch!

CODY: What am I telling all of this to you for? You don't even understand me.

*(*REED *feels around for where* CODY's *at. When he finds him, he holds* CODY's *hand.)*

REED: If she wants to stay, then you leave her dumb ass, and you never look back.

*(*CODY *looks at* REED. CODY *smiles.)*

CODY: Is that really you, Reed? Are you back with us?

REED: I never left. I was just acting. I even see clearer. You know what? I don't dream anymore. I haven't had a single dream since...since...since.... The dreams have stopped. No more bullshit. So I can only give you the truth.

CODY: What truth can you give me?

REED: Lena fucked the Butterman. *(Pause)* She sucked him off every chance she could get.

(Pause)

*(*CODY *kicks* REED *in the balls.* REED *slides to the floor, holding his groin.)*

(Pause)

(CODY *bends down and tries to comfort* REED.)

CODY: What the hell am I turning into?

REED: You're so damn blind. What are you turning into? You stay around here long enough and you can turn into a fucking flying monkey...a scarecrow.... Who knows? You could turn into a shadow.... Or, even your father.

CODY: I've told you before, you don't know a fucking thing about my father. People talking about my father...don't even know him....

REED: Did you know him?

CODY: What kind of question is that?

REED: We haven't got much time, Cody. Moms will be back in a minute. So I had to cut to the quick.

CODY: You want to cut to the quick? I wish I could be what my father was. There was a fucking man. You and Lena try to compare him to someone like to the Butterman? Okay, my father was a hustler...but see, he had a plan, Reed.... In his day, hustling was how some people made it up the ladder. For some of us, it was the only way we could become middle class. My father...he was from a different time and class of Butterman. By the time I was born he was fifty years old.... My old man, he ran with the big boys, the real mob. They let him run certain neighborhoods for them. They put apartment buildings and bars in his name. That's how much those Italians trusted him. They liked him, because he didn't act or talk like a nigger. Hell, he talked better than most of them. They liked him because he wasn't ostentatious.... He didn't go out and buy a fleet of Cadillacs, he didn't drink, gamble, or chase women.... Sometimes I'd ride around with my father.... We'd stop at diners and he'd meet dark-looking white men in cashmere coats and silk suits.... They'd hug him and kiss him on the cheek.... And I was this quiet little kid who just watched.... And they liked me, they used to say I was like my father... that I didn't say much, but I listened and observed....They liked that. Butterman is right this minute splattered against the pavement. What is he? Thirty-five? He's broke. So now his daughters have no father and no money. My dad, he

ACT TWO

was sixty-seven when he died. My mother doesn't have to worry about anything. When I'm twenty-five years old, I get money from a six-figure trust fund....That's a man that left a legacy. The Butterman left nothing.

REED: Yeah, but, thanks to you, the Butterman didn't live to be sixty-seven years old either.

CODY: That's a low blow, Reed.

REED: Bullshit. When you kicked me in the balls a few minutes ago, yo, Brother, that was a low blow.

(REED *laughs.* CODY *joins him.*)

REED: I like the sound of that.... Of your laughter.... We used to laugh and laugh all of the time. *(Pause)* It's not too late to get out.

CODY: I can't leave Lena here.

REED: Why you frontin', Cody? Why you dis' me this way? Or maybe you just frontin' on yourself.... See, this ain't got nothin' to do with Lena.

CODY: This has everything to do with Lena.

REED: Yo, Man, you need to dig yourself. You can't be so lame to think that she really loves you. I mean, you're square, but you ain't ever been slow.

CODY: You won't be so cynical about love once you've found that special person.

REED: Yo, the only woman I could even possibly, remotely love is myself in drag. Now you listen to me....

CODY: I haven't got time for this....

REED: Why? You got somebody else to toss out the window? Me maybe?

CODY: I wouldn't do that to you.

REED: Think about some of the things you've done this very night. You're turning cold-blooded. That's what this place does to you.

CODY: And what am I supposed to do?

REED: Get while the gettin's good, My Brother. If Lena really loves you like you say she does she'll find you....

CODY: And what about you?

REED: Fuck me! You got first blood on your hands, C. Run before it drowns you. This place gets in your blood, and when your blood comes from here.... I'd need a blood transfusion to get this shit out of me...but you can wash that shit off. But you've got to get out of here.

CODY: You mean just leave...how can I....

REED: Just click your ruby slippers together.... And let me tell you something, Cody, don't look back, for God's sake, whatever you do...don't even think about looking back.

(CODY *goes to the couch. He freshens his drink. He takes a sip.*)

CODY: You always know what's right.

REED: Then go. Do you want to wind up like me, or worse?

(CODY *sits down and takes another sip of his drink.*)

CODY: I'm leaving right now.

(LENORE, LENA, *and* JOB *return.*)

CODY: I'm gonna do it right now....

LENA: Who are you talking to, Cody?

(REED *slumps to the floor.*)

CODY: I'm trying to talk some sense into Reed.

LENORE: Too late for that.

(LENA *goes over to* REED *and hugs him.* CODY *takes another sip of his drink.*)

JOB: Will you look at this? I thought you were too good to take a drink. Lenore, how many times have I asked this boy to take a drink?... Mind if I have one with you?

CODY: Kill yourself.

(JOB *takes a glass from the table and pours a drink.* CODY *takes another sip.*)

LENA: What are you doing, Cody?

ACT TWO 79

LENORE: Let the man have his drink.

LENA: You've had enough, Cody.

(The bottle on the coffee table is empty now, so CODY gets up and goes to get the bottle on the dinette table. He pours some more, and then he sits down at the table. It is obvious that he is going rapidly past "high" into drunk.)

LENA: Did you hear me? That's enough.

CODY: Shut the fuck up! *(Pause)* Didn't you just see me kick ass and take names? I've got the juice. I am the serious, serious shit...if I want to be...so step off, Girl.

(LENORE looks at CODY for a beat.)

LENA: Who the fuck do you think you're talking to?

LENORE: I think you'd better leave this man alone.

CODY: See, Lena, Moms knows about men.

(LENORE goes over and pours herself a drink. Then she sits with CODY.)

CODY: So...how's the Prince?

LENORE: They just got through scapin' him off of the sidewalk. *(Pause)* By the way...congratulations...

(CODY gives her a puzzled look.)

LENORE: I'm going to be a grandmother at thirty-four. Imagine that.

CODY: I don't know what I'm going to do....

LENA: You said you'd work.

CODY: I do have my trust fund....

LENA: I'm not gonna wait four years for a trust fund...we've got to eat now.

(LENORE pulls a joint from her bosom and lights it. She takes a draw on it and then passes it to CODY. LENA gives an objectionable look. CODY smokes and talks.)

CODY: Lena's right, Moms, we need some money fast.

LENORE: You want to make it happen fast? *(Pause)* Hustle. *(Pause)* You've got some major talent running through your veins. Why let it go to waste? Niggers are always runnin' from what they is...instead of making something out of it.

CODY: I'm no hustler.

LENORE: I know, I know, I'm just saying.... If you know when to get out...a little scramblin' can get you on the good foot and even lead you to a life of class, dignity, and....

LENA: Money.

LENORE: Word the fuck up.

CODY: My mother would disown me.

LENORE: We wouldn't want that to happen. That would be terrible. Wouldn't it, Lena? *(LENA doesn't answer.)* But you know what I think? I think your mother would love you for it. If you went out there and carved out a little piece of something for yourself, without her help...well, if a son of mine did that I'd be just beamin' with motherly pride. Your mother is no different.

CODY: I don't know, Moms...hustling....

LENORE: You know what? It's wrong for me to be pressuring you like this. It's selfish.

(The joint has gone out. LENORE takes it out of his hand and relights it.)

CODY: You are far from selfish, Moms.

(She passes the joint back to him.)

LENORE: No, I'm the first one to admit when I'm wrong. I'm big like that.... See, I'm thinkin' 'bout my blood, all we've been through. All this family has ever known is projects and tenements. I once heard my Great-grandmother say that the last house this family ever lived in was a hut in Africa. I just want Lena to start her family...your family, in a real home.... But why should you have to fulfill my silly whims? But I do want you to remember something, Cody...hustling put your mother in the position she's in today. Hustling is in your blood. Your daddy made it from nothing. That's something to be proud of.

ACT TWO

CODY: You're right. My daddy, my dad...was a hell of a man.

LENORE: Yes he was.

CODY: I just proved tonight that it's in my blood....

LENORE: You certainly did.

CODY: So that must mean I'm a helluva fella too.

(CODY *looks around the room at everybody. He smiles. His head hits the table and bounces back up.*)

LENA: I told you he was too high, Moms.... Did you hurt yourself, Cody?

(CODY *drops his head back down on the table. This time it stays there.*)

LENA: Cody!

JOB: Don't worry, Sweets, he don't feel no pain.

LENORE: He sure will in the morning.

JOB: I hear that.

LENA: That supposed to be funny? Cody is not good at getting high.

LENORE: The boy got to learn sometime.

LENA: Maybe I don't want him to learn.

LENORE: Maybe it's no longer about what you want.

LENA: He's my man, it better be about what I want.

LENORE: What are you so upset about? I'm just tryin' to make sure the boy do you right.

LENA: I can take care of him....

LENORE: I've been dealin' with men longer than you and....

LENA: I'm the one who's pregnant, Moms, not you.

LENORE: I know that.

LENA: I just want you to remember that.

LENORE: What the hell does that mean?

LENA: Good night. *(She heads for the bedroom.)*

LENORE: What about your old man?

LENA: I don't sleep with drunks. *(She leaves.)*

LENORE: What a cold bitch. I don't understand how she can be so cold.

JOB: Got it from her father's side.

LENORE: You're right about that. That's exactly how her father's family got over. If I walked over everybody like they did just imagine where I'd be?

JOB: Tell me about it, Babes.... Well, I've got to be to work early, so I'm gonna crash.

LENORE: While you're at it, put Reed in his room.

(Taking REED with him, JOB leaves. LENORE stands over CODY.)

LENORE: You're comin' 'round, Boy.

(LENORE looks around, then she raises CODY's head and kisses him on the lips. He moans. LENORE gently places his head on the table. She laughs, pours herself another drink, and toasts CODY.)

(There is a knock at the door. She gulps down her drink and goes off stage to answer it. She returns with MARLENE rolling behind her in an electric wheelchair.)

MARLENE: How can anybody ride in that pissy elevator? *(She looks at CODY.)* You've drugged my boy.

LENORE: Yeah, he's wasted.

(MARLENE holds her chest—it is obvious that she's not feeling well.)

LENORE: So you finally rolled your crippled ass over here.

MARLENE: Don't you know anything about being civil?

LENORE: You gonna tell me you came over here to be civil? How'd you get over here?

MARLENE: I can drive you know.

LENORE: Can you now?

MARLENE: Where's Reed?

LENORE: He's bugged the fuck out. Now what the fuck do you want, Marlene?

ACT TWO

MARLENE: Cody's coming with me.

LENORE: Don't look like he's going no place to me. Looks like he's nice and comfortable...right at home.

MARLENE: Wake up, Cody. *(She rolls over to him and begins to shake him.)* Wake up you dumb cluck!

(He continues to sleep. LENORE laughs.)

LENORE: He was just having a little fun.

MARLENE: Wallowing in the gutter with you?

LENORE: All that's important is that Cody doesn't see us as trash. Now don't you come in my house with this uppity shit, 'cause you're from a hole in the wall just like me.

MARLENE: Look, all I want from you is my son.

LENORE: Shit, Cody ain't goin' no place. He's part of the family. See, Cody left a little nest egg in Lena, a little declaration of his love.

MARLENE: Ten to one, if we demand a blood test, we'll find out it's somebody else's.

LENORE: You watch what you say about my little girl.

MARLENE: Damn it, Cody, I tried to tell you this is the way trash operates.

LENORE: Who the fuck you callin' trash? I'm trash because I'm poor?

MARLENE: There's nothing wrong with being poor. Damn right, I come from poor people. Hell, most of us do. There's all kinds of trash out there, poor and rich. For example, you could live in the Taj Mahal, have a billion dollars in the bank, and you know, you'd still be walking, talking trash.

LENORE: Don't be tryin' to jerk me around with this superior shit....

MARLENE: You simply have no idea what I'm talking about. Yes, I'm superior to you, but it's not about money...it's about character....

LENORE: What the hell are you talking about?...

MARLENE: ...It's about pulling yourself up by your bootstrap.

LENORE: Yeah, I hear that bootstrap shit all the time from my caseworker.... Hell, I ain't never could afford no boot, much less a bootstrap....

MARLENE: Then you should have made one. If you would have learned to make your own boot, and you would have put that boot on, you wouldn't be on welfare today.

LENORE: What the fuck are you babbling about? What boots got to do with being poor? You know what, Girl? I think you been living around white people too long. And let me tell me somethin' 'bout them white neighbors of yours: When they see you comin' they see the same thing as when they see me. Let me tell you somethin' else, you have fucked with that boy's head with this uppitty bullshit so much that he don't even know who he is. You niggers from the suburbs are a fantasy...god damned TV shit. You don't belong there. That's right, I'm the first one to say it. If we're not born in a Coney Island most of us end up in one... because it's home. Word! It's the sho' nuff sho' nuff...and let me tell you this, in C.I., you don't have to worry about wakin' up to crosses burnin' on your lawn.

MARLENE: This is my son. My blood.

LENORE: One thing you got to realize, he ain't a baby no more, he's a man, he got responsibilities.

MARLENE: Isn't it enough that you ruined your own?

LENORE: Ruined? All my kids are fine.

MARLENE: Cody is mine. Do you think I'd let you ruin my bloodline? This boy is all I have in the world. He is what I lived for, so you better get it straight that I would die for him.

LENORE: What the fuck is your crippled ass gonna do? You better go home.... I don't appreciate people comin' in my house sellin' woof tickets.

(LENORE *turns and pours herself a drink.*)

(MARLENE *reaches into her purse and pulls out a pistol.*)

ACT TWO

(LENORE turns around and sees MARLENE aiming the pistol at her.)

MARLENE: This was my husband's pistol, he had it for a long, long time.... I don't believe he ever fired it.... But you know what he used to do? On Sundays, after church, he's sit in his den listening to jazz, and he'd clean this pistol until it sparkled. So even though I'm a hundred-percent sure that he never fired it, I'm just as sure that it's a well-greased machine that is...accurate.

(LENORE starts to move, but stops when MARLENE gives her a serious look.)

MARLENE: Cody's coming with me.

(They don't notice that CODY has awakened. He looks at the two women.)

LENORE: Why don't we leave that up to him.

MARLENE: I said he's going with me.

CODY: Bullshit, Ma.

(They both turn to look at him.)

CODY: I'm not going any place.

(Blackout)

Scene Two

(Six weeks later. The apartment. MARLENE is downstage. She sits there, paralyzed from the neck down. She can move her neck and eyes, but her mouth can barely move. To communicate, she makes grunting sounds. JOB is asleep on the couch. He is clutching a bottle of Dewar's. Outside the window the sky should indicate dawn. As the scene progresses, the sky should become brighter. CODY comes out with a glass of orange juice in hand. There is a straw in the glass. He is dressed in a blue, double-breasted, pin-striped suit. He is also wearing sunglasses. He kisses his mother.)

CODY: I'm worried about you, Ma. You haven't had much of an appetite lately....

(MARLENE *grunts.*)

CODY: I know, I know...food looks less appetizing when it's mashed up like baby food.

(*He brings the glass to his mother's face. Then he slips the straw between her lips.*)

(*She does not drink.*)

CODY: Come on, Ma, it's good for you.

(*She drinks.* CODY *looks at his watch. She stops drinking. He puts the glass on the dinette table. He goes to the window and looks out. He looks at his watch again. He comes back down to his mother.*)

(*Pause*)

CODY: Remember how you used to straighten my tie?... (*He straightens it himself.*) How do I look?

(*She grunts and makes other sounds.*)

CODY: I'm so edgy. This meeting...and everything else happening today.... (*He takes a half pint of Dewar's from his jacket pocket. He takes a swig.* MARLENE *groans in protest. He puts the bottle back in his jacket.*) Maybe a walk on the beach will calm me down. (*He kisses* MARLENE *on the cheek and leaves.*)

(*A beat passes.* REED *comes in from the bedroom area. He is feeling his way with his cane. Shades still cover his gouged-out eyes. In his other hand is a can of lighter fluid. He makes his way to where* MARLENE *is.*)

REED: I've got the answer right here.

(*He places the can where he thinks her face is.* MARLENE *looks at* REED.)

REED: They're all asleep.... This is the best way. When it's all over, Cody will see.

(MARLENE *starts grunting and groaning as passionately as she can in her condition. There is absolute fear in her eyes.*)

REED: My sentiments exactly...but think of it...we'll be singing "Ding dong the Bitch is dead" all the way to the Emerald City.

ACT TWO

(MARLENE's *grunting grows harsher.*)

(REED *starts soaking the carpet, the couch,* MARLENE, *and, finally, his head and clothes. He puts the can down.*)

(LENORE *comes in and looks around. She picks up the can of lighter fluid.*)

(REED *takes out matches.* LENORE *sneaks up behind him.* REED *lights a match.* LENORE *softly blows it out.* REED *drops the match to the floor. He waits for the flames.*)

(*Pause*)

(REED *sniffs for smoke. He lights another match, and starts to raise it above his head. As he does,* LENORE *blows it out again.* REED *places a match on his hair. He braces himself for the human torch he thinks he is about to become. After a beat, he feels his hair.*)

REED: Where's the fire?

LENORE: Up your ass!

(LENORE *kicks him in the butt.* REED *falls to the floor on his hands and knees.*)

LENORE: I knew you was frontin'...and now I've caught your ass red-handed.

REED: When I saw the mountains I just didn't know what to do....

LENORE: Don't even try that shit...your card has been peeped, Little Nigger!

REED: ...then I saw the stars...they were MGM Technicolor Munchkins and I wanted to be amongst them...and so I had to climb, climb, climb.

(LENORE *kicks him.* REED *begins to crawl across the floor.* LENORE *kicks him again. He is now at the foot of* MARLENE's *wheelchair. He clings to it.*)

REED: Even if the climb took forever, he vowed to keep on, for he knew that if he reached the mountain he would be saved....

(LENORE *pushes her knee into his back.* REED *cries out in pain.*)

LENORE: You need your balls cut off and your brains cut out!

(She bites his hands, which are wrapped around the wheelchair. REED screams, baby-like.)

REED: Mama. Mama, Mama, Mama....

LENORE: You jive-ass nigger, you was jerkin' us.

(JOB springs up awake in a half-drunken stupor. LENA enters in her robe. LENA and JOB rush over to pull LENORE off REED.)

JOB: Whatcha tryin' to do, Babes?

LENORE: He's been layin' in the cut all the time...just pretendin' to be bugged.

LENA: Come on, Moms, you know the doctors said Reed would never be straight again.

JOB: What the boy do?

LENORE: Can't you smell it? Can't you see the floor is soaked with lighter fluid?

(LENA bends down and feels the carpet.)

LENORE: That blind demon was about to barbecue us alive.

LENA: Calm down, Moms.

LENORE: Calm the-fuck-down? I save all our lives, and now y'all are trying to make me out to be the bitch? Where's the appreciation?

JOB: We appreciate you, Babes.

LENA: But you've got to understand, Reed is insane....

REED: Watch out for the poppy fields!

LENORE: Insane? Niggers are always tryin' to cop a plea. Insanity...that's white people shit. They are the only ones who can get away with that. Ain't a damn thing wrong with Reed. Just needs an old-fashioned ass kicking.

LENA: He can't help himself.

LENORE: You can believe that if you want to, all I know is, I don't want the sucker in my house.

JOB: He's your son.

ACT TWO

LENORE: Listen here, the kids are coming back from camp this morning, why should they have to deal with his crazy ass?

LENA: Please, Moms, let him stay. *(Pause)*

(LENORE goes to the bedroom area. JOB heads for the coffee table, where he picks up the bottle of Dewar's he was sleeping with. There is about a half-shot left in the bottle.)

JOB: Damn. *(He turns the bottle up and finishes it.)* This ain't doin' jack-shit for me.

(He goes to the window and looks out. He begins to shake. He looks at his arm. He smacks it.)

(LENA goes over and tries to comfort REED.)

REED: I can see! I can see!

LENA: Poor Reed.

(LENORE enters with a dog leash, dog collar, and extension cord.)

LENA: What are you going to do to him?

LENORE: You want him to stay?

(LENA gets out of LENORE's way.)

(LENORE puts the collar around REED's neck. REED feels the dog collar. He attempts to crawl away, but LENORE catches him by the back of his pants. She sits on him. The impact knocks the breath out of him. LENORE ties his hands behind his back with the extension cord. She then snaps the leash to the collar, then ties the leash to the wheelchair. LENORE rises and kicks REED. REED whimpers.)

(JOB turns from the window.)

JOB: Damn it, I need a drink.

LENORE: What you want me to do? It's six-thirty in the morning.

(JOB begins shaking and twitching.)

JOB: You're my woman, you're supposed to make me happy.

LENORE: You got that shit ass-backwards.... And that's just why you don't have a wake-up drink.

JOB: I ain't been happy lately....

LENORE: You ain't been much of a man lately.

JOB: If you cared.... Wanted me....

LENORE: Maybe if *I* was happy.

JOB: What about me? *(Pause)* What the fuck about me?

LENORE: What about you?

(Silence)

(Still trembling, JOB *sits in a dinette chair.)*

JOB: Roaches... We're gettin' more and more of 'em 'round here.... They gettin' bigger and bigger....

*(*LENORE *and* LENA *look, but they see no roaches.)*

LENA: He's getting sick, Moms.

*(*JOB *slaps imaginary bugs off himself. He stops and looks around.)*

LENORE: He's fakin'.

LENA: Faking?

LENORE: Don't you know that's the pastime of black men?

JOB: I'm all right. I just don't know where all the roaches came from...how they got so big....

LENA: I don't think he's faking.

LENORE: After this afternoon you'll know what I mean.

LENA: This afternoon?

LENORE: You'll be married. That's when men really start fakin'. *(Pause)* Boy, you're so cool...even forgot you was gettin' married today. If I was in your shoes, I'd be tremblin'....

LENA: No big thing, Moms. I just wish I wasn't carrying this baby.

LENORE: Only six or seven more months. Consider it insurance.

ACT TWO   91

(JOB *has drifted off to sleep in the chair.*)

LENA: You think Cody is making the right move with the money?

(MARLENE *grunts.*)

LENORE: With me schoolin' him? And with the power of attorney he has over all that long green....

(MARLENE *groans.*)

LENORE: We'll get over like fat rats in the streets. Look ahere, your old man is gonna be the King of Coney Island.

(CODY *enters.*)

LENORE: Here comes my son-in-law to be.

CODY: Morning, Moms.

(CODY *comes across the room.* LENA *starts to go to him for a kiss, but* CODY *bypasses her to go* LENORE. *He gives* LENORE *a hug and a brief kiss on the lips.*)

LENA: Where were you?

CODY: I went for a walk down on the boardwalk. All the way to the She-Ape exhibit. You know, it's like we never worked there...now that I've become the serious shit.

LENORE: You certainly are the serious shit.

(CODY *looks at* REED *tied to the wheelchair.*)

CODY: Why is Reed chained like a dog?

LENORE: He tried to set fire to the place.

CODY: What?

LENORE: I say he was fakin' all along, but Lena and Job say he's insane. So I had no choice.

(*Pause*)

(CODY *studies* REED *close.* REED *sniffs. Then he spits in the direction he thinks* CODY *is in. He hits* CODY'S *shoes.*)

CODY: Insane...absolutely insane. (*Pause*) Look, if you want me to put him away somewhere....

LENA: You'd put my brother away?

LENORE: I wouldn't let you waste your money. If push come to shove we'll let the welfare take care of it.

CODY: Whatever you want, Moms.

LENA: What about what I want?

LENORE: It's going to be somethin' else havin' you in the family.

(LENA steps up to CODY, but CODY continues to look at LENORE.)

CODY: I'm just grateful for the kindness you've shown me and my mother....

LENA: Who's your woman here? Do you hear me? I'm right here in your face...in your motherfucking face. Don't you ig' me...don't you dis' me....

CODY: If I didn't know better I'd think you were on your period.

(CODY tries to kiss her, but she evades him. He starts to go to her, but LENORE catches him by the hand and pulls him to her. She begins to straighten his tie.)

LENORE: You're not nervous, are you.

CODY: To tell the truth, I was a little earlier this morning. But I really have nothing to worry about, you really schooled me about the way it is.

LENA: You black fuck, I hate your sorry ass.

CODY: Excuse me for a moment, Moms.

(He starts for LENA, then he stops, goes into his pocket, and takes out a vial of cocaine.)

CODY: I almost forgot. *(He hands it to LENORE.)* A sample of the product.

LENORE: This is the shit?

(LENORE goes over to the dinette table. She opens the vial and begins to snort.)

(CODY tries to grab LENA and kiss her.)

LENA: Get off of me.

ACT TWO

(She claws at CODY, *scratching him. He backhands her. She reels back, more shocked than hurt.* CODY *is just as surprised.)*

CODY: Do you know who you're fucking with?

LENA: Yeah, somebody who can't fuck.

*(*CODY *pounces on her. He slaps her in the head and twists her nose. He then tosses her on to the couch. He hovers over her, almost shocked at his own behavior.)*

CODY: Lena, I'm sorry...I....

(She tries to hit him. He hits her. She covers up. He stops hitting her, but she is still covered up. He hovers over her.)

(Silence)

(The sound of LENORE *snorting the coke.* LENA *is sobbing.)*

LENORE: This is better than anything the Butterman ever thought about. You gonna have every bitches' nose in C.I. wide-the-fuck-open. They'll be droppin' their panties left and right.

CODY: Hmmmmm.

*(*LENA *is sobbing.)*

CODY: I shouldn't have been so rough on her.

LENORE: Oh come on...those were love taps. Are her eyes black, is her nose broken?... You just gave her what she wanted, a little attention.... Hey, ain't it about time she picked up the kids.

CODY: What time does the camp bus come in?

LENORE: Seven-thirty.

*(*CODY *looks at his watch. He walks over to* LENA. *She covers her head.)*

CODY: I think you should go pick up your brothers and sisters.... Did you hear me?

LENA: I have to get dressed.

(She exits. JOB *begins to stir in his sleep.)*

JOB: They comin' to eat me. *(He screams.)* They chewin' the shit out of me. *(He laughs in his sleep.)*

LENORE: Shut the fuck up.

CODY: He's just having a dream.

LENORE: He don't have a damn thing to dream about. If he got dreams that mean he ain't workin' hard enough. *(Pause. She looks* CODY *over.)*

LENORE: Damn, you look good.... If you weren't my daughter's nigger.... But then I'm old....

CODY: Thirty-four is not old, Moms.

LENORE: I feel old. I'm chained to this can't-get-it-up-sucker. My face is scarred for life....It's depressing.

CODY: Let me show you how I make Lena feel good. You see, I have this thing about multiple vitamins.

LENORE: Are you jerkin' me?

CODY: Vitamins do for me what acid does for Reed.

LENORE: Get out of town.

CODY: I'll prove it to you. *(He goes to the entrance of the bedroom area.)* Lena...bring me my vitamins. *(Pause)* I hope for your sake that you're not thinking about ignoring me. *(He goes back to* LENORE.*)* Now don't worry, I've got it all under control.

LENORE: Got what under control?

CODY: You'll see.

*(*LENA *comes out fully dressed. She stands there with the bottle of vitamins.)*

LENORE: This fool is trying to tell me that he gets high off of vitamins.

LENA: You're going too far, Cody.

CODY: It's just a goof, Baby Girl. I want to cheer Moms up.

LENA: Can't you find some other way?

CODY: Give me the bottle, and just maybe I won't slap you into your next period.

(Pause)

(She gives CODY *the bottle. He kisses her on the forehead.)*

ACT TWO

LENA: This was our thing...our joke....

CODY: And now we can share the fun with your mother. Now why don't you make yourself useful and pick up your brothers and sisters.

LENORE: And while you're at it, you can take Reed for a walk.

CODY: And you know what else, Baby Girl? It would be really sweet if you took my mother out for a little morning sun, too.

LENORE: I think Marlene would like that.

(MARLENE *groans.*)

LENORE: Sure you would.

LENA: Where's Reed's cane?

LENORE: If you don't want him pullin' some wack shit on you, you'd better keep him on the leash.

(LENA *looks at* CODY *and* LENORE *for a beat. She unties* REED *from the wheelchair. She leaves, pushing* MARLENE *in the chair, and pulling* REED *by the leash.*)

LENORE: That bitch is a trip.

CODY: No, these are.

(CODY *opens the vitamins and pops a couple in his mouth. He stands there for a few beats.*)

LENORE: What are you doin', Fool?

(CODY *looks at her slippers and begins to shake.*)

CODY: Tell them to stop, Moms.

LENORE: Tell who to what?

CODY: Your slippers, they're laughing at me.

LENORE: Cut this silly shit.

CODY: I wish I could...but when the multiple vitamin power hits my system.... Well, I'm not to be held responsible. Please! Tell them to stop.

(CODY *drops to his knees. He starts to bark at* LENORE's *slippered feet.* LENORE *tries to keep a straight face, but finally she explodes into laughter.*)

LENORE: Get out of here, Boy...

CODY: Then make them stop.

(CODY *bangs his fists at* LENORE's *feet as if he's trying to smash them intentionally.* LENORE, *not sure if he's playing or not, begins to move her feet in order to avoid his fists.* CODY *grabs one of her legs and begins to hang on to it as she tries to wiggle away. Her slipper comes off and he begins to playfully bite her foot.*)

LENORE: Stop it...that tickles....

CODY: Tell them to stop.

(*He howls like a wolf. She falls to the floor. They laugh.*)

CODY: See, I got you to smile.

LENORE: You're something else.

CODY: So are you... (*Pause. They kiss. Pause.*)

(CODY *pushes her to the floor and gets on top of her. He starts ripping off her night clothes. He pulls up her slip, then unbuckles his pants. He takes her hand and puts it inside his pants. They kiss.*)

CODY: I've always wanted a woman like you.

LENORE: Get out of here... (*She giggles.*)

CODY: Straight up.

LENORE: Go on...

CODY: It's true...I always wanted a woman who could get down.

LENORE: That's me.

CODY: There's something incredibly sexy....

LENORE: Yes...

CODY: About women who can sweat...(*Pause*) About ghetto women...(*Pause*) About cheap women...

LENORE: Cheap?

ACT TWO

(She tries to push him off but he holds on to her.)

CODY: That's what it is...the cheapness. Like when I see some girl on Mermaid Avenue in a halter top and tight shorts...there's something about her.... She's nothing like the girls where I come from.... It's not the body, it's the face...a certain low-class look.... A cheapness that makes me horny.... All street women have this look.... It's in the faces of whores all over the city.

LENORE: Whores? I ain't nobody's whore.

CODY: Lena told me that you used to be....

LENORE: That's because I had to....

CODY: Whoring is whoring.... You're cheap, Lenore, but I like it...I love it.

LENORE: Don't run this shit on me...

CODY: Stop frontin', Lenore.... Just open your legs and say "Ahhh".

(LENORE pushes CODY off and gets up.)

LENORE: You jive-ass son of a bitch.

CODY: I'm only telling you the truth. You dig the truth don't you? The real deal? Straight up? On the one? *(Pause)* You're a cheap ex-whore...and the beauty of it is that you'll never be anything else. And you know it...and you don't try to hide it. I find that very sexy.

LENORE: So I'm a cheap whore?... Word!... Thank you for reminding me. Sometimes I run a Murph on myself...the serious scam....

CODY: You mean you dream?

(CODY pulls her down on the couch, then gets on top of her.)

LENORE: You dead on, I will never be anything more than what I am...an ex-whore-junkie-wino-child-desertin'-roughhouse-cut-your-fucking-throat-in-a-second bitch.

CODY: You feel so weak....

LENORE: I don't need you to read me. I can read myself.

CODY: I bet your knees are like jelly right now.

LENORE: But let me read you this: You remind me of what I am...but I hope you remember who I am. Don't you ever forget it. Now, I done schooled you, Nigger...and I want my share.

CODY: I'm the one with the balls here. I'm the one on top. You don't think I'm going to let the likes of you touch my parents' hard-earned money?

LENORE: The likes of me? I schooled you, Nigger.

CODY: And I'll thank you for it...every time I'm between your legs.... Now I'll pass you some crumbs, I'll take care of y'all, but my way.... Now are we going to talk business or take care of business?

(He shoves her back on the couch.)

LENORE: Now look ahere...

(He rips off her underwear.)

CODY: You don' have to give it to me, I'm gonna take it....

(JOB wakes up, screaming. LENORE pushes CODY off and jumps up. JOB begins beating off invisible attackers.)

JOB: Get 'em off me, Babes!

CODY: He's bugging. *(He laughs.)*

LENORE: He needs a drink. Cut the shit, Job.

JOB: They're tryin' to eat me, Babes....

CODY: You know what he needs?

LENORE: I know exactly what he needs.

(LENORE goes to the kitchen. JOB continues to freak out. CODY laughs. LENORE returns with the meat cleaver. She waves it in front of JOB's face.)

LENORE: Job, sit your ass down. I'll get you a drink soon as the liquor store opens.

(JOB drops to the floor and goes under the kitchen table. CODY laughs as he sits on the couch.)

LENORE: My husband ain't for your entertainment.

ACT TWO

(CODY *pulls the half-pint of scotch from his pocket. He opens it and takes a sip.*)

(Pause)

LENORE: Motherfucker.

CODY: You're the mother. I'm the fucker.

LENORE: That's some cold shit. You see the man goin' through changes, and you sit there with the cure in your pocket.

CODY: That was some funny shit. Besides, a sip of this won't put him, or you, out of misery.

LENORE: Me?

(CODY *walks over to the dinette table.*)

CODY: What are you going to do with this miserable lame?

LENORE: Don't you be judgin' my husband.

CODY: A woman like you...keeping this old juice fiend.

LENORE: He's a hell of a man.

CODY: Is that why you want to get your rocks off with me?

LENORE: He saved my life.... He once was a hell of a man. He still is sometimes.

CODY: Ask me if I give a damn.

(CODY *waves the bottle in front of* JOB's *face.* JOB *crawls out from under the table. He reaches for the bottle;* CODY *jerks it away. He pours the rest of the bottle on* JOB's *head. He then picks up the lighter fluid and pours the rest of it on* JOB.)

LENORE: What do you think you're doin'.... You're fixin' to get killed....

(CODY *pulls out a book of matches.*)

LENORE: Cut it, Cody, or I'll....

CODY: Or you'll what? Who do you think you're talking to? Job? It can't be the sweet, sweet Butterman. He's not going to rise from the dead. *(Pause)* I see your shit, Lenore. Can you dig it? I know what a good fuck does to you. Shit, between the sheets you're just like all the other bitches. So cut the hardrock-lady-Bogart-bullshit. Your games don't work on a man like me.

(CODY *looks down at* JOB. JOB *is shaking again.*)

CODY: I've got the sure-enough hell-fire cure, Job.

(*As* CODY *is about to strike the match,* LENORE *grabs him by one arm. A slow-motion sequence begins as she slowly guides the meat cleaver between his legs.* CODY *is in shock as he falls to the floor, bleeding.*)

(LENORE *stands over him.*)

(*Then, she drops the meat cleaver, and goes to* JOB, *who is on the floor in front of the table.*)

LENORE: Job...I think I'm in trouble....

JOB: They won't eat you, Babes....

LENORE: You don't understand...I think I did it this time.

JOB: Don't you worry about a thing, Babes...

LENORE: But, Job...

JOB: Just keep 'em from eatin' me, and I'll keep 'em from eatin' you....

(*The lights fade slowly on this tableau.*)

www.ingramcontent.com/pod-product-compliance
Lightning Source LLC
Chambersburg PA
CBHW071723040426
42446CB00011B/2187